GREAT
WRITING 2

Great Paragraphs

FOURTH EDITION

KEITH S. FOLSE
UNIVERSITY OF CENTRAL FLORIDA

APRIL MUCHMORE-VOKOUN
HILLSBOROUGH COMMUNITY COLLEGE

ELENA VESTRI SOLOMON
KHALIFA UNIVERSITY OF SCIENCE, TECHNOLOGY,
AND RESEARCH, UAE

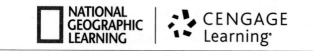

NATIONAL GEOGRAPHIC LEARNING | CENGAGE Learning

Australia • Canada • Mexico • Singapore • Spain • United Kingdom • United States

Great Writing 2: Great Paragraphs
Keith S. Folse, April Muchmore-Vokoun,
Elena Vestri Solomon

Publisher: Sherrise Roehr

Executive Editor: Laura Le Dréan

Development Editor: Charlotte Sturdy

Director of Global Marketing: Ian Martin

International Marketing Manager:
Caitlin Thomas

Director of Content and Media Production:
Michael Burggren

Senior Content Project Manager: Daisy Sosa

Senior Print Buyer: Mary Beth Hennebury

Cover Design: Christopher Roy and Michael
Rosenquest

Cover Image: JOEL SARTORE/ National
Geographic Stock

Interior Design: Aysling Design

Composition: PreMediaGlobal, Inc.

U.S. Edition

ISBN-13: 978-1-285-19490-5

International Student Edition

ISBN-13: 978-1-285-75060-6

National Geographic Learning
20 Channel Center Street
Boston, MA 02210
USA

Cengage Learning is a leading provider of customized learning solutions with office locations around the globe, including Singapore, the United Kingdom, Australia, Mexico, Brazil, and Japan.

Cengage Learning products are represented in Canada by Nelson Education, Ltd.

Visit National Geographic Learning online at **ngl.cengage.com**

Visit our corporate website at **www.cengage.com**

Printed in the United States of America
3 4 5 6 7 8 9 19 18 17 16 15

Contents

Scope and Sequence

Unit	Writing	Grammar for Writing	Building Better Vocabulary	Original Student Writing
1 p. 2 **PARAGRAPHS**	• What Is a Paragraph? • Four Features of a Paragraph • Working with Paragraphs	• Using the Simple Present Tense with Facts • Using the Imperative in Process Paragraphs • Using the Simple Past Tense in Narrative Paragraphs • Checking for Verbs and Fragments	• Word Associations • Using Collocations	**Original Student Writing:** Write a paragraph of your choice. **Photo Topic:** Write about something thrilling. **Timed Writing Topic:** Describe the daily life of a police officer.
2 p. 32 **DEVELOPING IDEAS FOR WRITING A PARAGRAPH**	• Brainstorming • How Brainstorming Works	• Subject-Verb Agreement	• Word Associations • Using Collocations	**Original Student Writing:** Write a paragraph of your choice. **Photo Topic:** Write about something very scary. **Timed Writing Topic:** Is English easy or difficult to learn?
3 p. 46 **TOPIC SENTENCES**	• The Topic Sentence • Features of a Good Topic Sentence	• Using Commas in Sentences • Avoiding Three Common Sentence Errors	• Word Associations • Using Collocations	**Original Student Writing:** Brainstorm and write a paragraph about animal communication, international flights, pollution, or smart phones. **Photo Topic:** Write about learning something new. **Timed Writing Topic:** Why do so many people want to learn English?
4 p. 70 **SUPPORTING AND CONCLUDING SENTENCES**	• Supporting Sentences • Concluding Sentences	• Using Pronouns in Place of Key Nouns	• Word Associations • Using Collocations	**Original Student Writing:** Write a paragraph of your choice. **Photo Topic:** Write about a place to visit in your town or city. **Timed Writing Topic:** Is it a good idea to require all students to wear a school uniform?

Unit	Writing	Grammar for Writing	Building Better Vocabulary	Original Student Writing
5 p. 94 **PARAGRAPH REVIEW**	• Review • Working with the Structure of a Paragraph • Analyzing Paragraphs	• Reviewing Articles	• Word Associations • Using Collocations	**Original Student Writing:** Write a paragraph of your choice. **Photo Topic:** Write about something interesting to do. **Timed Writing Topic:** What are the best snack foods?
6 p. 116 **DEFINITION PARAGRAPHS**	• What Is a Definition Paragraph? • Quotation Marks • Putting the Paragraph Together: Sequencing	• Using Adjective Clauses • Creating Sentences with Variety	• Word Associations • Using Collocations	**Original Student Writing:** Write a definition paragraph. **Photo Topic:** Define an emotion. **Timed Writing Topic:** What does the word courage mean to you?
7 p. 138 **PROCESS PARAGRAPHS**	• What Is a Process Paragraph?	• Using Sequence Words and Chronological Order	• Word Associations • Using Collocations	**Original Student Writing:** Write a process paragraph. **Photo Topic:** Write about a process or how something happens. **Timed Writing Topic:** What are the steps in correcting an error on a bill?
8 p. 154 **DESCRIPTIVE PARAGRAPHS**	• What Is a Descriptive Paragraph? • Describing with the Five Senses • Using Positive and Negative Adjectives for More Precise Meanings	• Using Adjectives in Writing • Using Prepositions of Location to Describe • Using Correct Word Order with Prepositions of Location	• Word Associations • Using Collocations	**Original Student Writing:** Write a paragraph that describes something. **Photo Topic:** Describe a national monument that is important to you. **Timed Writing Topic:** Describe your ideal teacher.
9 p. 180 **OPINION PARAGRAPHS**	• What Is an Opinion Paragraph? • Facts and Opinions • Topic Sentences for Opinion Paragraphs • Choosing a Topic for an Opinion Paragraph	• Recognizing Word Forms and Common Suffixes	• Word Associations • Using Collocations	**Original Student Writing:** Write an opinion paragraph. **Photo Topic:** Write your opinion about the best kinds of zoos. **Timed Writing Topic:** What minimum age should be required to get a driver's license?

(Continued)

Unit	Writing	Grammar for Writing	Building Better Vocabulary	Original Student Writing
10 p. 198 **NARRATIVE PARAGRAPHS**	• What Is a Narrative Paragraph? • Working with Ideas for Narrative Paragraphs	• Maintaining Verb Tense Consistency	• Word Associations • Using Collocations	**Original Student Writing:** Write a narrative paragraph about an experience that you have had. **Photo Topic:** Write about a surprising, frightening, happy, or funny experience you have had. **Timed Writing Topic:** Write about a specific event from your childhood.
11 p. 222 **PARAGRAPHS IN AN ESSAY: PUTTING IT ALL TOGETHER**	• From Paragraphs to Essays • Getting to Know Essays • What Does an Essay Look Like? • Putting an Essay Together		• Word Associations • Using Collocations	**Original Student Writing:** Write a narrative, comparison, cause-effect, or argumentative essay. **Photo Topic:** Write about the effect of technology in rural places. **Timed Writing Topic:** What should happen to students who are caught cheating on an exam?

Overview

Framed by engaging **National Geographic** images, the new edition of the *Great Writing* series helps students write better sentences, paragraphs, and essays. The new *Foundations* level meets the needs of low-level learners through practice in basic grammar, vocabulary, and spelling, while all levels feature clear explanations, student writing models, and meaningful practice opportunities. The new edition of the *Great Writing* series develops academic writing skills for learners at all levels.

> *Great Writing: Foundations* focuses on basic sentence construction, emphasizing grammar, vocabulary, spelling, and composition.
>
> *Great Writing 1* focuses on sentences as they appear in paragraphs.
>
> *Great Writing 2* teaches paragraph development.
>
> *Great Writing 3* transitions from paragraphs to essays.
>
> *Great Writing 4* focuses on essays.
>
> *Great Writing 5* practices more advanced essays.

The earliest ESL composition textbooks were merely extensions of ESL grammar classes. The activities in these books did not practice English composition as much as they did ESL grammar points. Later books, on the other hand, tended to focus too much on the composing process. We feel that this focus ignores the important fact that the real goal for English learners is both to produce a presentable product and to understand the composing process. From our years of ESL and other L2 teaching experience, we believe that the *Great Writing* series allows English learners to achieve this goal.

Great Writing 2: Great Paragraphs offers introductory material on paragraph writing. The book is designed for intermediate students; however, the language is controlled as much as possible so that dedicated upper beginners and weak advanced students may also benefit from the instruction. Depending on the class level and the amount of writing that is done outside of class, there is enough material for 60 to 80 classroom hours. If a more substantial amount of writing is done outside of class, the number of hours for a faster group can be as little as 40.

Organization

In *Great Writing 2*, Units 1–5 deal with the elements of a good paragraph. Units 6–11 feature five different kinds of paragraphs and an introduction to writing essays. While it is not necessary to cover these five paragraph modes in the given order, the current sequencing will allow for some recycling of grammatical and lexical items. *The Brief Writer's Handbook with Activities* and the *Appendices* contain additional practice material to support both the process and the mechanics of writing.

Contents of a Unit

Although each unit has specific writing objectives (listed at the beginning of the unit), the following features appear in every unit:

Example Paragraphs

Because we believe that writing and reading are inextricably related, the 101 example paragraphs model a rhetorical mode and/or provide editing activities. Many models are often preceded by schema-building questions and are followed by questions about organization, syntactic structures, or other composition features. New, potentially unfamiliar vocabulary words are glossed next to each paragraph. These words can provide students with a list of vocabulary to add to a separate vocabulary notebook.

Grammar for Writing

Since good writing requires good knowledge of the mechanics of English, *Great Writing* includes clear charts and detailed instruction that relates directly to the writing assignments. In addition, numerous activities give students the opportunity to practice and refine their grammar and writing knowledge and skills.

Activities

The new, fourth edition contains more than 150 activities, 55 suggestions for additional paragraph writing assignments and 31 supplemental activities in the *Brief Writer's Handbook with Activities*. These writing, grammar, and vocabulary activities gradually build the skills students need to write well-crafted sentences and paragraphs and provide learners with more input in English composition, paragraph organization, and cohesion.

Building Better Vocabulary

Each unit includes two vocabulary-building activities to build schema and collocations. In the first activity, Word Associations, the student identifies words that best relate to the target vocabulary word. This allows them to build connections to more words and thus grow their vocabulary more quickly. Words from the Academic Word List are starred (see pages 275–276 for the complete list). The second activity, Using Collocations, helps students learn specific word combinations, or collocations, which will help their original writing sound more advanced. It is helpful to encourage students to use these new words in their Original Student Writing assignment and to add them to a vocabulary notebook.

Writer's Notes

Great Writing 2: Great Paragraphs features small pieces of writing advice that help writers understand more about use and format. Content includes brainstorming techniques, peer editing guidelines, citing original sources, and plagiarism.

Building Better Sentences

Periodically in each unit, students are asked to turn to Appendix 1 and work on building better sentences. Each practice is intentionally short and includes only three problems. In each problem, there are three to five short sentences that the students must combine into a single sentence that expresses all the ideas in a logical and grammatically correct manner.

Original Writing

Each unit includes an activity that requires students to do some form of writing. *Original Student Writing* includes writing prompts and a set of directions to encourage students to follow the writing process and refer back to the lessons taught in the unit.

Additional Writing Topics give students the opportunity to continue practicing their writing skills. The first topic always links back to the opening photograph and writing prompt. It is up to the teacher to decide whether all students will write about the same topic or if each student is free to choose any of the topics listed.

Peer Editing

At the end of each unit, a peer editing activity offers students the opportunity to provide written comments to one another with the goal of improving their paragraphs. A unique peer editing sheet for each unit can be found online at NGL.Cengage.com/GW2, and each one provides the guidance and structure that is necessary for students at this level to successfully perform this task. We recommend that students spend 15 to 20 minutes reading a classmate's paragraph and writing comments using the questions on the peer editing sheet.

Timed Writing

One way to improve students' comfort level with the task of writing under a deadline, such as during a testing situation, is to provide them with numerous writing opportunities that are timed. The final activity in each unit features a timed-writing prompt that is geared toward the grammar and sentence structure presented in that unit. Students are given five minutes to read the prompt and make a quick writing plan, followed by 25 minutes of actual writing. Instructors may use this activity at any time during the lesson.

What's New in This Edition?

- Engaging images from **National Geographic** connect learning to the greater world.

- New and updated readings act as springboards and models for writing.

- Updated Grammar for Writing sections clearly present grammar and help students learn the structures for writing.

- Streamlined instruction and practice activities offer step-by-step guidelines to focus writers on both the writing process and product.

- Words from the Academic Word List are highlighted in vocabulary activities, encouraging students to expand their word knowledge.

- The expanded *Brief Writer's Handbook* now includes a Useful Vocabulary for Writing section to help writers choose appropriate language for the different rhetorical modes.

- An all-new level, *Great Writing: Foundations* introduces students to the basics of grammar, spelling, and vocabulary.

- A new Online Workbook encourages learners to further practice grammar, vocabulary, and editing skills. Students can also write paragraphs or essays, and submit them to the instructor electronically.

- An updated Presentation Tool allows instructors to use the book in an interactive whiteboard setting and demonstrate the editing process.

- An eBook provides another option to use *Great Writing* in a traditional or blended learning environment.

Ancillary Components

In addition to the *Great Writing 2: Great Paragraphs* Student Book, the following components help both the instructor and the students expand their teaching and learning.

- **Online Workbook**: Includes a wealth of vocabulary, grammar, writing, and editing practice with immediate feedback.

- **Presentation Tool CD-ROM**: Offers instructors the ability to lead whole-class presentations and demonstrate the editing process.

- **Assessment CD-ROM with ExamView®**: Allows instructors to create and customize tests.

- **Teacher Companion Site at NGL.Cengage.com/GW2**: Provides teachers with answer keys, peer editing sheets, and teacher's notes.

- **Student Companion Site at NGL.Cengage.com/GW2**: Provides students with peer editing sheets, glossary, and interactive flashcards.

- **eBook**: Offers an interactive option.

Inside a Unit

Great Writing 2:
Great Paragraphs

Framed by engaging **National Geographic** content, the new edition of the *Great Writing* series helps students write better sentences, paragraphs, and essays. The new *Foundations* level meets the needs of low-level learners through practice in basic grammar, vocabulary, and spelling, while all levels feature clear explanations, student writing models, and meaningful practice opportunities. The new edition of the *Great Writing* series develops academic writing skills for learners at all levels.

Unit
1 Paragraphs

GOAL: To learn the four main features of a paragraph
To use the correct form for verbs in a paragraph

A carnival ride throws off orbs of light in St. Paul, Minnesota.

2

Impactful **National Geographic** images provide engaging topics to encourage student writing.

Over 100 Sample Writing Models focus on specific writing skills and rhetorical modes.

Vocabulary words are glossed to encourage independent mastery of new terms.

ACTIVITY 2 Reading Example Supporting Sentences

Read the paragraphs on pages 73–75. Notice how the supporting sentences tell you more about the topic sentence. Compare what you wrote in Activity 1 to the information in each paragraph. How well did you predict the content?

Example Paragraph 21

A Great Tourist Destination

New York and Boston attract millions of tourists, but I think one of the best cities to visit on the east coast of the United States is Washington, D.C. It has some of the most interesting **landmarks** and tourist **spots** in the country. There are many monuments to visit, such as the Lincoln Memorial, the Jefferson Memorial, and the Washington Monument, which is the tallest building in Washington. For more excitement, the area called Georgetown in northwest Washington is famous for its shopping and restaurants. Finally, there is the White House tour. On this tour, the guide **leads** visitors as they walk through many of the rooms in the White House and **view** the home of the president of the United States. Although Washington, D.C., does not have the large number of visitors that New York or Boston does, I think this city is one of the best destinations for tourists.

a landmark: a historical building, a well-known location

a spot: a place, a location

to lead: to show the way, organize

to view: to see, look at

73

Grammar for Writing

Using Pronouns in Place of Key Nouns

Because a paragraph is about one topic, writers often repeat key nouns from the topic sentence in their supporting sentences. However, too much repetition of these same nouns can sound awkward. You can avoid repeating key nouns by replacing them with **pronouns** after the nouns are first introduced.

Explanation	Examples
Pronouns take the place of a person, place, or thing: Carla → She Washington → It Giraffes → They Replace nouns with pronouns to avoid repetition.	One of the best cities to visit on the east coast of the United States is **Washington, D.C. It** has some of the most interesting landmarks and tourist spots in the country. One of the people that I most admire is **my great-grandmother Carla. She** came to the United States from Italy in 1911 as a young woman on a large ship.
Remember to be consistent. If you use *they* at the beginning of a paragraph, do not switch to *it*. The underlined words are incorrect in the example.	**Giraffes** are among the most interesting of all the animals that live in Africa. **They** are easily recognized by **their** special features. **They** have long necks and long legs, but its neck is longer than its legs. It usually lives in very dry areas.

ACTIVITY 9 Identifying Key Nouns and Pronouns

Read the following sentences. Write the correct pronoun in each blank. Use *it, they,* or *we*. Then underline the key noun that the pronoun refers to.

1. Tennis rackets have changed tremendously in the last ten years. ___They___ used to be small and heavy, but that is no longer true.

2. Soccer is by far the most widely played sport in the world. _____ is played professionally on nearly every continent.

3. I will never forget my childhood friends Carlos and Juan and what _____ taught me.

4. Not only is text messaging fast, but _____ is also an interesting way to practice English.

5. A bad thing happened to my classmates and me at school yesterday. _____ were late coming to class, so the teacher gave us an extra homework assignment.

6. If you travel to Budapest, Hungary, you will fall in love with the Danube River. _____ separates the city into two parts—Buda and Pest.

> New **Grammar for Writing** sections provide clear explanations and examples of the target grammar, giving learners easy access to the structures they will use in their writing.

> **Guided, structured activities** help students practice writing, grammar, and editing skills.

> **Building Better Vocabulary** activities highlight words from the Academic Word List and prompt students to apply their vocabulary and knowledge of collocations.

Building Better Vocabulary

ACTIVITY 10 Word Associations

Circle the word or phrase that is most closely related to the word or phrase on the left. If necessary, use a dictionary to check the meaning of words you do not know.

	A	B
1. to plagiarize	to follow	to steal
2. a surge	less	more
3. to reject*	to say *no*	to say yes
4. to quote*	to destroy something	to repeat something
5. bland	tasteless	tasty

Original Student Writing: Opinion Paragraph

ACTIVITY 11 Original Writing Practice

Develop a paragraph about a strong opinion that you have. Include facts to support your opinion. Follow these guidelines:

• Choose a topic such as the value of living abroad, connecting teachers' salaries to students' grades, or why young children need their own cell phones.

• Brainstorm your topic. If you want, use the Internet for ideas.

• Write a topic sentence with a controlling idea.

• Write supporting sentences with facts that support your opinions.

• Check for incorrect word forms.

• Use at least two of the vocabulary words or phrases presented in Activity 9 and Activity 10. Underline these words and phrases in your paragraph.

If you need ideas for words and phrases, see the Useful Vocabulary for Better Writing on pages 275–279.

> **Original Student Writing** gives students the chance to combine the grammar, vocabulary, and writing skills together in one writing piece.

> **Peer Editing** activities increase students' awareness of common errors.

Timed Writing

How quickly can you write in English? There are many times when you must write quickly, such as on a test. It is important to feel comfortable during those times. Timed-writing practice can make you feel better about writing quickly in English.

1. Take out a piece of paper.

2. Read the writing prompt.

3. Brainstorm ideas for five minutes.

4. Write a short paragraph (six to ten sentences).

5. You have 25 minutes to write your paragraph.

In your opinion, why do so many people want to learn English? Give a few strong examples to support your answer.

> **Timed Writing** prepares students for success on standardized and international writing exams.

For more practice with the grammar, vocabulary, and writing found in this unit, go to NGL.Cengage.com/GW2.

Technology   *Great Writing 2*

For Instructors:

The Presentation Tool CD-ROM contains time-saving, interactive activities from the student book, a set of whiteboard tools, and additional content to help the instructor guide learners through the editing process.

Teacher's Notes, Answer Keys, and Peer Editing Sheets are available online for instructors.

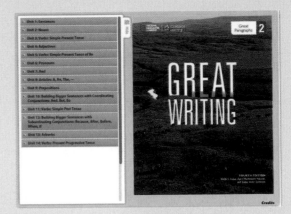

The Assessment CD-ROM with ExamView® allows instructors to create and customize tests and quizzes easily.

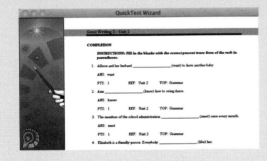

For Students:

The Online Workbooks: Each level features additional independent practice in vocabulary, grammar, writing, and editing.

***Great Writing* eBooks** are available for all levels and are compatible with tablets, laptops, and smartphones.

Acknowledgements

We would like to thank the hundreds of ESL and English composition colleagues who have generously shared their ideas, insights, and feedback on second language writing, university English course requirements, and textbook design.

We would also like to thank Laura Le Dréan, Thomas Jefferies, Ian Martin, and Emily Stewart from National Geographic Learning for their guidance. We are extremely grateful for the support given to us by our developmental editors Katherine Carroll, Charlotte Sturdy, and Yeny Kim. We also remain forever grateful to our previous editors at Houghton Mifflin, Susan Maguire, Kathy Sands-Boehmer, and Kathleen Smith for their indispensable guidance throughout the birth and growth of this writing project.

Likewise, we are indebted to the following reviewers who offered ideas and suggestions that shaped our revisions:

Laura Taylor, Iowa State University, Iowa
Mary Barratt, Iowa State University, Iowa
Abdelhay Belfakir, University of Central Florida, Florida
Taoufik Ferjani, Zayed University, United Arab Emirates
Cheryl Alcorn, Pasadena City College, California
Paul McGarry, Santa Barbara City College, California
Fernanda Ortiz, University of Arizona, Arizona
Michelle Jeffries, University of Arkansas—Fayetteville, Arkansas
Suzanne Medina, California State University—Dominguez Hills, California
Kristi Miller, American English Institute, California
Kevin Van Houten, Glendale Community College, California
Izabella Kojic-Sabo, University of Windsor, Canada
Wayne Fong, Aston School, China
Yiwei Shu, New Oriental School, China
Raul Billini, John F. Kennedy Institute of Languages, Dominican Republic
Rosa Vasquez, John F. Kennedy Institute of Languages, Dominican Republic
Mike Sfiropoulos, Palm Beach State College, Florida
Louise Gobron, Georgia State University, Georgia
Gabriella Cambiasso, City College of Chicago—Harold Washington, Illinois
Lin Cui, Harper College, Illinois
Laura Aoki, Kurume University, Japan
Rieko Ashida, Konan University, Japan
Greg Holloway, Kyushu Institute of Technology, Japan
Collin James, Kansai Gaigo University, Japan
Lindsay Mack, Ritsumeikan Asia Pacific University, Japan
Robert Staehlin, Morioka University, Japan
Jenny Selvidge, Donnelly College, Kansas
Phan Vongphrachanh, Donnelly College, Kansas
Virginia Van Hest Bastaki, Kuwait University, Kuwait
Jennifer Jakubic, Century College, Minnesota
Trina Goslin, University of Nevada—Reno, Nevada
Margaret Layton, University of Nevada—Reno, Nevada
Amy Metcalf, University of Nevada—Reno, Nevada
Gail Fernandez, Bergen Community College, New Jersey

Lynn Meng, Union County College—Elizabeth, New Jersey

Zoe Isaacson, Queens College, New York

Sherwin Kizner, Queens College, New York

Linnea Spitzer, Portland State University, Oregon

Jennifer Stenseth, Portland State University, Oregon

Rebecca Valdovinos, Oregon State University, Oregon

Renata Ruff, Prince Mohammed University, Saudi Arabia

Ya Li Chao, National Taichung University of Science and Technology, Taiwan

Kuei-ping Hsu, National Tsing Hua University, Taiwan

Morris Huang, National Taiwan University of Science and Technology, Taiwan

Cheng-Che Lin, Tainan University of Technology, Taiwan

Rita Yeh, Chia Nan University of Pharmacy and Science, Taiwan

Nguyen Chanh Tri, Vietnam Australia International School, Vietnam

Mai Minh Tien, Vietnam Australia International School, Vietnam

Tuan Nguyen, Vietnam Australia International School, Vietnam

Nguyen Thi Thanh The, Vietnam Australia International School, Vietnam

Nguyen Vu Minh Phuong, Vietnam Australia International School, Vietnam

Colleen Comidy, Seattle Central Community College, Washington

Cindy Etter, University of Washington, Washington

Kris Hardy, Seattle Central Community College, Washington

Liese Rajesh, Seattle Central Community College, Washington

Finally, many thanks go to our students who have taught us what ESL composition ought to be. Without them, this work would have been impossible.

Keith S. Folse
April Muchmore-Vokoun
Elena Vestri Solomon

Photo Credits

Paragraphs

The bungee slingshot thrills tourists
in Singapore.

Can you write about a thrilling event or sport?

What Is a Paragraph?

A **paragraph** is a group of sentences about one topic or one idea. Learning to write a paragraph is an important academic skill. On the next few pages, you will find three example paragraphs—a comparison paragraph, a process paragraph, and a narrative paragraph. Each example shows what a good paragraph looks like.

ACTIVITY 1 Studying an Example Paragraph

This paragraph is about two countries that are near each other but have many differences. Discuss the Preview Questions with your classmates. Then read the paragraph and answer the questions that follow.

Preview Questions

1. What are some things you could compare about two cities or countries?

2. What things do you know about Brazil and Chile?

Example Paragraph 1

Chile and Brazil

Chile and Brazil are two important countries in South America. **Although** they are near each other, they are very different in **geography**, population, and language. The easiest difference to see is in geography. Brazil is much larger than Chile. In fact, Brazil is the largest nation in South America and **takes up** almost half of the **entire** South American continent. Brazil is so large that it shares a **border** with every South American country except Chile and Ecuador. In contrast, Chile is a very **narrow** country along the Pacific Coast of South America. The widest point in this long country is only 160 miles (258 kilometers). These two countries also **differ** in population. Brazil is home to almost 200 million people, but only about 17 million people live in Chile. Finally, these two countries differ in national languages. Like most countries in South America, the **majority** of people in Chile speak Spanish. In Brazil, however, the most commonly spoken language is Portuguese because the Portuguese **settled** in Brazil in 1500. These three differences make these countries extremely interesting.

although: contrast between two ideas; but

the geography: the land of a place

to take up: occupy space

entire: whole, all

a border: a line between two countries

narrow: the opposite of wide

to differ (in): be different

the majority: more than half

to settle: to come to live in a new area

Brazil

Chile

Post-Reading

1. Which three things are being compared here?

_____

2. In your own words, what are the two biggest differences? Begin your sentence like this: "The two biggest differences between ..."

_____

_____

3. Make a list of three other things you know about each of these countries. (Interview classmates or consult the Internet if necessary.)

Country 1: _____	Country 2: _____
1.	1.
2.	2.
3.	3.

Grammar for Writing

Using the Simple Present Tense with Facts

Explanation	Examples		
Use the **simple present** to explain something that is still true today. It is a general fact.	These two countries also **differ** in population. The majority of people in Chile **speak** Spanish.		
The simple present uses the **base form** of the verb for *I, we, they,* and *you,* and the **–s form** for *he, she,* and *it* and other third person nouns. The subject must agree with the verb in number (singular or plural).	I / We / They / You / Brazilians	**speak**	**Portuguese.**
	He / She / It / The man	**speaks**	

Look at Example Paragraph 1 on page 4 and answer the questions.

1. Draw two lines under each verb. What tense are most of the verbs? _____

2. One verb is in the simple past. Write it here. _____

3. Why is this verb in the simple past? _____

Writer's Note

Repetition

Look again at the Example Paragraph 1 on page 4.

- How many sentences are there in the paragraph? _____

- How many times is the word *Brazil* the subject of a sentence? _____

- How many times is the word *Chile* the subject of a sentence? _____

The words *Brazil* and *Chile* are repeated often because this is the topic that is being explained and described. Repetition of key nouns is sometimes necessary to avoid confusion. For example, if we use the word *it* five or six times in this paragraph, we might not know if we are talking about Brazil or about Chile.

ACTIVITY 2 Writing Practice

Think of something that is unique about you. It can be about your hobby, language, or family. Write five sentences about that topic. What verb tense will you use?

1. _____

2. _____

3. _____

4. _____

5. _____

Studying an Example Paragraph

A process paragraph tells how to do something. Discuss the Preview Questions with your classmates. Then read the paragraph and answer the questions that follow.

Preview Questions

1. Can you cook? What are three things that you can cook by yourself?

2. Who taught you how to prepare them?

Example Paragraph 2

An Easy Sandwich

An egg salad sandwich is one of the easiest and most delicious foods to make for lunch. First, **boil** two eggs for five minutes. Take them out of the water and let them cool off. Next, **peel** away the **shells** and put the eggs into a bowl. Use a fork to **mash** them very well. After that, add three tablespoons of mayonnaise. Add a little salt and pepper. Mix these **ingredients** well. Put the egg salad in the refrigerator for **at least** thirty minutes. Just before you are ready to eat, **spread** the egg salad on bread. If you follow all these steps, you will certainly enjoy your creation.

to boil: to cook in water at 212°F (100°C)

to peel: to take away the outside covering

a shell: the outside covering of an egg

to mash: to push down and break into small pieces

the ingredients: the parts to make something

at least: the minimum number or amount of something that is required

to spread: to move something in many directions

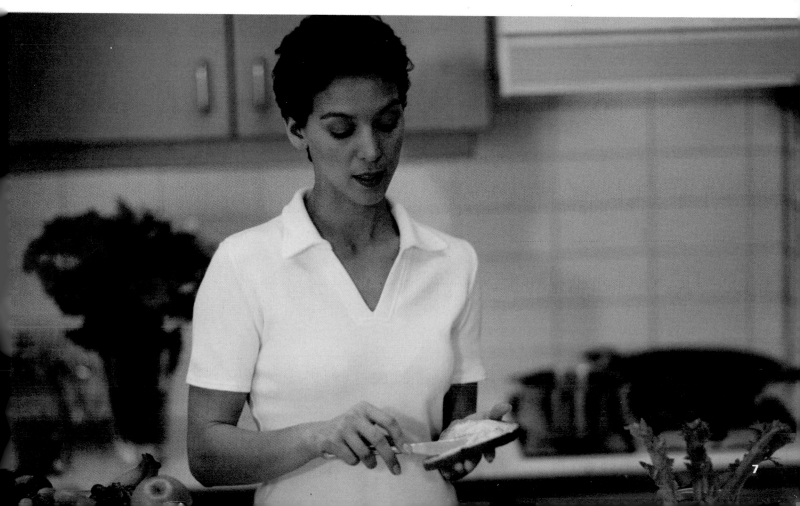

Post-Reading

1. What is the main purpose of this paragraph? (Why did the author write this paragraph?)

    _____

    _____

    _____

    _____

2. Do you know another easy recipe? Write the main steps of the recipe. Tell it to your classmates and then listen to your classmates present their recipes.

    _____

    _____

    _____

    _____

    _____

    _____

    _____

    _____

    _____

Grammar for Writing

Using the Imperative in Process Paragraphs

Imperative sentences give directions or commands.

Explanation	Examples
Use the **base form of the verb** to begin an imperative sentence.	**Mix** these ingredients well.
When you give written directions, the **sequence** or order of the steps is important. Add a **sequence word** before the imperative. Sequence words include *First, Second, Third, Next, Then,* and *Finally*. Remember to add a comma after a sequence word or phrase.	**First,** boil two eggs for five minutes. **Next,** peel away the shells.

Look at Example Paragraph 2 on page 7 and answer the questions.

1. How many sentences are there in "An Easy Sandwich? " _____

2. Circle the 15 main verbs in the sentences.

3. How many sentences begin with an imperative? _____

4. How many sentences begin with a sequence word? _____

ACTIVITY 4 **Writing Practice**

Think of a process that you know how to do. Write four to seven sentences that explain how to complete that process. For example, you can write about food or an everyday routine (e.g., how to bake bread or how to send a text message). Use imperative sentences and sequence words.

1. _____

_____

2. _____

_____

3. _____

_____

4. _____

_____

5. _____

_____

6. _____

_____

7. _____

_____

ACTIVITY 5 **Studying an Example Paragraph**

Can you remember a time when you had a strong feeling about something? Perhaps you were happy or sad or angry. In the narrative paragraph on the next page, the writer tells about a day when he was afraid. This emotion was so strong that he remembers many details about the event even though it took place many years ago. Read the paragraph and answer the question that follows.

My First Flight

Although the first time I flew on a plane was many years ago, I can still remember how afraid I was that day. All my life, I had **wondered** what it would be like to fly in an airplane. Finally, in March of 1990, I **boarded** my first flight. I flew from New Orleans, Louisiana, to Managua, Nicaragua, on SAHSA Airlines. It was a Boeing 727 jet. There were three seats on each side of the **aisle**. It was **sort of** crowded, and this only made me more nervous. Every time we hit a little **turbulence**, my hands **turned** white. I was so nervous during the **entire** flight that I did not eat the meal they gave me. I would not even go to the bathroom. I cannot tell you how **relieved** I was when the plane finally landed at our **destination**. Since then, I have been on **over** one hundred flights, but I can still remember many small **details** of my first airplane flight.

to wonder: to ask yourself about something, to imagine what something is like

to board: to get on a plane (or other form of transportation)

an aisle: the row between seats on a plane (or bus or train)

sort of: somewhat, rather

the turbulence: rough air during a flight, bumpiness

to turn: to change, become

entire: complete, whole

to be relieved: the feeling when a person no longer feels pressure about something

your destination: the final place that you are traveling to

over: more than

a detail: a fact about something

Post-Reading

Almost everyone has traveled by plane. Can you remember your first flight? Write three questions to ask a classmate about his or her first flight. Then work in small groups and take turns asking each other your questions.

1.   *What do you remember about your first flight?*
   _____

2. _____
   _____

3. _____
   _____

Grammar for Writing

Using the Simple Past Tense in Narrative Paragraphs

Writing a story about something that has happened is called **narrative** writing. Most verbs in narrative writing are in the simple past.

Explanation	Examples
Use the simple past to tell a story or event that happened in the past. Form the past by adding **-d** or **-ed** to the base form of the verb.	I **boarded** my first flight. He **lived** in Chile.
Many verbs have **irregular past** forms. Be sure to check a dictionary to find the correct form.	go → went begin → began eat → ate have → had

1. Underline all the verbs in "My First Flight." How many verbs are there? _____

2. How many of the verbs are in the simple present tense? _____

3. How many of the verbs are in the simple past tense? _____

ACTIVITY 6 **Writing Practice**

Think of something that happened to you, such as a funny event or a happy occasion. Write five to eight sentences in which you tell the story.

1. _____

2. _____

3. _____

4. _____

5. _____

6. _____

7. _____

8. _____

Building Better Sentences: For further practice with the sentences and paragraphs in this part of the unit, go to Practice 1 on page 284 in Appendix 1.

Four Features of a Paragraph

These are the four main features of a paragraph:

1. A paragraph has a topic sentence that states the main idea.

The topic sentence is usually at the beginning and is the foundation for the paragraph. The topic sentence helps the reader understand what the paragraph is about. (Topic sentences will be discussed more in Unit 3.)

2. All of the sentences in a paragraph are about one topic.

They are connected to the topic sentence. There are no unrelated or extra sentences. How do you know whether something is connected or not? Look at the main idea in the topic sentence, which is sometimes called the *controlling idea*. All of the other information in the paragraph must be connected to the controlling idea in the topic sentence. (You will learn more about this in Unit 3 on page 46.)

3. The first line of a paragraph is indented.

Indenting means moving the first line to the right about a half of an inch. On a keyboard, this is about six spaces or the first tab stop position. This gap, or open space, in the first line is called an indentation.

4. The last sentence, or concluding sentence, brings the paragraph to a logical end.

The concluding sentence usually states the main point again or summarizes the main idea of the paragraph. Often a key word or phrase from the topic sentence appears in the concluding sentence. In addition, it can offer a suggestion, an opinion, or a prediction. (Concluding sentences will be discussed more in Unit 4.)

ACTIVITY 7 **Analyzing the Features of a Paragraph**

Discuss the Preview Questions with your classmates. Then read the paragraph and answer the questions that follow.

Preview Questions

1. Do you have a pet?

2. Who cares for the pet? What kind of care does it need?

Example Paragraph 4

Children and Pets

At some point, most parents have to decide whether or not to **allow** their children to have pets. Some parents believe that pets teach children **a sense of** responsibility because children have to learn how to take care of their pets. In addition, many parents believe that pets can be fun for the family. Pets can also help children become more **compassionate** because children will develop a special **bond** with their pets. **On the other hand**, some parents are afraid that their children might hurt the animals or that these animals might hurt the children. Cats are good pets, but I do not like it when they shed hair **all over**. Often these parents do not allow their children to have any kind of pet. Other families do not have the extra time or money that pets **require**. In **brief**, although many children want a pet, parents are divided on this issue for **a number of** important reasons.

to allow: to permit, let

a sense of: a feeling of

compassionate: with strong feelings of caring or wanting to help

a bond: a connection, a relationship

on the other hand: an expression used for the second or opposite reason ("on one hand" versus "on the other hand")

all over: everywhere

to require: to need, must have

brief: short

a number of: several

Post-Reading

1. What is the main idea of the paragraph?

   many Parents are undecided on unther
   are not to allow then chillen to have a
   pet

2. How many sentences are there in the paragraph? _9_

3. How many sentences do NOT relate to the main idea? _0_ Draw a line through any unrelated sentences.

4. Draw a line under the topic sentence. (Remember that the topic sentence is the sentence that helps the reader understand the main idea.)

5. Is this paragraph indented? ☑ yes ☐ no

6. Draw two lines under the concluding sentence. How is the information in the concluding sentence related to the information in the topic sentence?

   _____

   _____

ACTIVITY 8 Analyzing the Features of the Example Paragraphs

Look at these three example paragraphs again: "Chile and Brazil" on page 4, "An Easy Sandwich" on page 7, and "My First Flight" on page 9. Fill in the information about the features of each paragraph.

1. Write the topic sentence of each paragraph.

   "Chile and Brazil" _____

   _____

   "An Easy Sandwich" _____

   _____

   "My First Flight" _____

   _____

2. What is the main idea of each paragraph?

   "Chile and Brazil" _____

   "An Easy Sandwich" _____

   "My First Flight" _____

3. Is the first line of each paragraph indented?

"Chile and Brazil"   ❑ yes ❑ no

"An Easy Sandwich"   ❑ yes ❑ no

"My First Flight"   ❑ yes ❑ no

ACTIVITY 9 **Analyzing the Features of Student Paragraphs**

Read the following student paragraphs and answer the questions that follow.

Example Paragraph 5

eBook Readers

eBook readers are excellent **devices** for students. Reading eBooks is just like reading a **normal** book without having to hold the book or turn the pages. These devices save students energy. Before eBook readers, students had to carry many heavy books with them each day. However, eBook readers are **extremely** lightweight and usually weigh less than a pound. eBook readers are more **efficient** and

an eBook: an electronic book

a device: a small machine or instrument

normal: usual

extremely: very

efficient: capable or productive

convenient than a regular book. They are wireless, so students can use them anywhere. They are comfortable to hold and are clear even in bright sunlight. My friend has an eBook reader, and she **convinced** me to buy one. Finally, **purchasing** a new book for an eBook reader is simple and cheap. There are now millions of eBooks available, and many eBooks cost less than **traditional** books. It is clear that eBook readers have certainly made students' lives much easier.

to convince: persuade

to purchase: buy

traditional: normal or usual; not new

1. The general topic of the paragraph is how eBook readers help students. Does the paragraph have a topic sentence? If so, write it here. If not, create one here.

   eBook readers are excellent devices for students.

2. Are all the sentences related to the topic? If not, write the unrelated sentences here.

   My friend has an eBook reader, and she convinced me to buy one.

3. Is the first line indented?   ☑ yes ☐ no

4. What is the concluding sentence?

   It is clear that eBook readers have certainly made students' lives much easier.

Example Paragraph 6

Simón Bolívar

Simón Bolívar (1783-1830) was one of South America's greatest generals and one of the most powerful people in world political history. In Spanish, Simón Bolívar is often called *El Libertador*, which means "The Liberator." Spanish is the **principal** language in at least 22 countries. This **nickname** is a very good one because his planning and military actions helped to gain independence from Spain for six countries: Bolivia (1809), Colombia (1819), Ecuador (1820), Panama (1821), Peru (1821), and his native country of Venezuela (1811). In fact, Bolivia is named for Bolívar, making him one of the few people to have a country named for him. These six countries together are **approximately** the same size as modern Europe, so the independence of such a large area was an amazing military and political **feat**. Although Bolívar's name is not as well-known outside Latin America, people there remember him as perhaps the most important person in their history.

the principal: main, the most important

a nickname: a short name that people use in place of a longer name

approximately: about, more or less

a feat: an accomplishment

Post-Reading

1. What is the topic of the paragraph? _Simón Bolívar_

   Does the paragraph have a topic sentence? If so, write it here. If not, create one here.

   Was one of South American's greatest general.

2. Are all the sentences related to the topic? If not, write the unrelated sentences here.

   Bolivia 1709, Colombia 189, Ecuador 1820, etc

3. Is the first line indented? ☑ yes ☐ no

4. What is the concluding sentence?

   Although Bolívar's name is not as well-known outside Latin America ... etc.

17

New York City

First, many movies were made here, so people have seen the city even if they have not traveled here in person. Second, New York City has many famous tourist attractions, including the Statue of Liberty, the Empire State Building, Central Park, and Times Square. In addition, the city has some of the best shopping in the world, and many famous department stores are located here. Finally, New York City is famous for its many theaters with world-class shows. For these reasons, everyone knows about this city.

Post-Reading

1. What is the topic of the paragraph? _NEW YORG CITY._

   Does the paragraph have a topic sentence? If so, write it here. If not, create one here.
   NEW YORK CITY IS QUERY KNOW CITY.
   WHY NEW YOUR IS FAMOUS ?

2. Are all the sentences related to the topic? If not, write the unrelated sentences here.
   YES.

3. Is the first line indented?   ☑ yes ❏ no

4. What is the concluding sentence?
   FOR THESE REASON, EVERYONE KNOWS
   about this CITY.

Jim Thorpe's Final Victory

Jim Thorpe is a **controversial** figure in sports history. He won Olympic gold medals for running in 1912, but he was not allowed to keep them. In the 1912 Olympics, Thorpe won both the pentathlon (five events) and decathlon (ten events). However, a month later, the U.S. Olympic Committee took away his medals because Thorpe had played baseball for money. An athlete who takes money for sports is called a professional, and at that time, professional athletes were not allowed to **take part in** any Olympic Games. In 1982, the U.S. Olympic Committee **reversed** this **ruling**. Seventy years **after** his **achievements**, Thorpe's name was finally returned to the list of 1912 Olympic winners.

controversial: causing great disagreement or discussion

to take part in: to participate in

to reverse: to change to the opposite position

a ruling: a decision, especially one that is made by a judge or court

an achievement: something special that a person is able to accomplish or do

Post-Reading

1. What is the topic of the paragraph? _Olympic Game._

   Does the paragraph have a topic sentence? If so, write it here. If not, create one here.

   Jyes ?

2. Are all the sentences related to the topic? If not, write the unrelated sentences here.

   yes

3. Is the first line indented? ☑ yes ☐ no

4. Underline the concluding sentence. Do you see any time words in the concluding sentence that make the sentence sound like the ending of the paragraph?

   Seventy years after, Finally.

Reasons for Not Voting

Although voting is one of the main ways that people of a country can participate in their future, some **citizens** choose not to vote. Some people decide not to vote because they think that their one vote will not matter. Other people do not vote because they are not interested in politics. Another reason that some people choose not to vote is that they do not know much about politics or **politicians** and do not have enough time to learn about them before an election. Finally, in some elections, people choose not to vote because they do not like any of the **candidates** in the election. People's reasons for not voting **vary considerably**.

a citizen: a legal member of a city, state, or country

a politician: someone who holds a government office

a candidate: a person running for political office

to vary: to be different

considerably: a great deal, by a large amount

Post-Reading

1. What is the topic of the paragraph? Reason For not voting

   Does the paragraph have a topic sentence? If so, write it here. If not, create one here.

   YES, it DOES

2. Are all the sentences related to the topic? If not, write the unrelated sentences here.

   YES

3. Is the first line indented? ☑ yes ☐ no

4. What is the concluding sentence?

   People's reasons For not voting vary considerably.

Example Paragraph 10

My First Class as a Teacher

I can still remember a small **incident** that helped me relax on my first day of teaching many years ago. I was 23 years old at the time, and I had just graduated from college. The practice teaching that I had done for six weeks was very different from teaching my own class. When I walked into the room, I was very nervous. I carefully put my books down on the desk. Then I heard a girl say something in Spanish to another classmate. I speak Spanish, so I understood her perfectly when she told her friend to look at my hands. She said, "Look how his hands are **trembling**," and she was right. I was wearing a new watch that day, too. **Neither** of the two girls knew that I could understand Spanish. When I smiled a little, the first girl started to laugh because she realized at that moment that I understood Spanish. It seems like such a **silly** thing now, but the **humor** of the incident really helped me relax on the first day of my **career**.

an incident: a small event, usually negative

to tremble: to shake

neither: not A and not B (used with two choices)

silly: funny, crazy

the humor: funny part

a career: what a person does for a living

21

Post-Reading

1. What is the topic of the paragraph? _The writers as a theactik_.

   Does the paragraph have a topic sentence? If so, write it here. If not, create one here.

   yes, it DOES

   _____

2. Are all the sentences related to the topic? If not, write the unrelated sentences here.

   no. I was weaving a new water
   that day, too.

3. Is the first line indented? ☑ yes ☐ no

4. Underline the concluding sentence.

5. What words are repeated in both the topic sentence and the concluding sentence of this paragraph?

   helped me relax on my frist day of.

Building Better Sentences: For further practice with the sentences and paragraphs in this part of the unit, go to Practice 2 on page 285 in Appendix 1.

Working with Paragraphs

In this section, you will begin to learn about organizing and formatting a paragraph by copying sentences into paragraphs and then by writing a paragraph of your own. You will also look at good titles for paragraphs.

ACTIVITY 10 **Reviewing Capitalization and End Punctuation**

Review "Basic Capitalization Rules" on page 254 and "End Punctuation" on pages 257–258 in the *Brief Writer's Handbook with Activities*. Add correct capitalization and end punctuation to the sentences below. If you need more practice, complete the activities on pages 255–258.

1. the geography of the country of turkey is unique

   The geography of the country of Turkey is unique.
   _____

2. most countries are in one continent, but turkey lies in both asia and europe

   _____

3. the asian part is much larger than the european part

   _____

4. the eight countries that share a border with turkey are armenia, azerbaijan, bulgaria, georgia, greece, iran, iraq, and Syria

   _____

5. turkey has coasts on the mediterranean sea and the black sea

   _____

6. half of turkey's land is higher than 1,000 meters

   _____

7. in fact, two-thirds of turkey's land is higher than 800 meters

   _____

8. the unique geography of turkey is one reason that millions of tourists visit this country every year

   _____

ACTIVITY 11 **Copying a Paragraph**

Copy the sentences from Activity 10 in the same order. Make sure your paragraph is indented. Write a title on the top line.

Example Paragraph 11

_____

_____

_____

_____

_____

_____

_____

_____

_____

_____

_____

_____

_____

_____

The Title of a Paragraph

What is the title of this textbook? Look on the front cover. Write the title here.

_____

What is the title of Example Paragraph 11 on page 24? Write the title here.

_____

A **title** tells you what you will find in a book, a movie, a story, or a paragraph. A title is not a sentence. A title is usually very short. Sometimes the title is only one word, such as the movie titles _Spiderman, Batman,_ or _Titanic._ Can you think of other movie titles in English that are only one or two words long?

A good paragraph title is catchy. It has something that catches the reader's interest, but it does not tell everything about the paragraph. As an example, imagine that you wrote a paragraph about a time when you burned some scrambled eggs. Consider these titles.

Title	Comment
I Burned the Eggs	Poor title. A title should not be a sentence.
Burning the Eggs	Poor title. The meaning is not accurate. This sounds like you will tell how to burn the eggs.
Cooking Scrambled Eggs	Poor title. The meaning is not accurate. This sounds like you will tell only how to cook scrambled eggs.
A Bad Experience with Scrambled Eggs	This is a little better, but it is not clear if this is about eating eggs or making eggs.
The Day I Tried to Make Scrambled Eggs	This is acceptable if the paragraph tells the events of that day.
A Cooking Disaster	Good title. It sums up the paragraph but does not tell exactly what happened.
A Kitchen Disaster	Good title. It sums up the paragraph but does not tell exactly what happened.

Grammar for Writing

Checking for Verbs and Fragments

Look at the **verbs** in these examples.

Explanation	Examples
Every sentence in English must have a verb. When writing, always check or proofread each sentence to make sure it has a verb!	✓ Where **is** the bank? ✓ Wheat **is grown** in Argentina. ✓ Japan **produces** many different kinds of cars. ✓ The house on the corner **does** not **have** a garage. ✓ Two amazing buildings in the United Arab Emirates **are** the Burj Al Arab and the Dubai Tower.
A sentence without a verb is called a **fragment.** The word *fragment* means a piece of something that has been broken off.	✗ Where the bank? ✗ Japan many different kinds of cars. ✗ Wheat in Argentina. ✗ The house on the corner not a garage. ✗ Two amazing buildings in the United Arab Emirates the Burj Al Arab and the Dubai Tower.

You will study more details about sentence fragments in Unit 3 on page 62.

ACTIVITY 12 **Checking Subjects and Verbs**

Read each sentence. The subject is in *italics*. Underline the verb that goes with each subject. If every subject in the sentence has a verb, write C for correct on the line. If a subject does not have a verb, write X on the line and add an appropriate verb in the correct place. (Many different verbs can be used. Use one that you think is appropriate.)

1. ___**X**___ We know that *languages* vary, but other important communication *methods* ^exist.

2. ___C___ For example, when two *people* are talking, the appropriate *amount* of space between them varies by culture.

3. ___X___ In some cultures, *people* ^stand near each other when having a conversation.

4. ___C___ Sometimes these *people* might touch each other during the conversation.

5. ___C___ *Not standing near the speaker or not touching* might be seen as "cold" or disinterested behavior.

6. ___C___ In other cultures, *people* stand farther apart.

7. ___X___ If *one* of the speakers *is* too close, the other *person* might see this as aggressive or strange behavior.

8. ___X___ The *amount* of personal space *varies* from culture to culture.

9. ___X___ It *is* also a form of communication.

10. ___C___ Just as there is no universal *language,* there is no universal personal *space.*

Copying a Paragraph

Copy the sentences with your corrections from Activity 12 in the same order. Make sure your paragraph is indented. On the top line, write an original title for your paragraph.

Example Paragraph 12

_____

_____

_____

_____

_____

_____

_____

_____

_____

_____

_____

_____

_____

Building Better Vocabulary

ACTIVITY 14 **Word Associations**

Circle the word or phrase that is most closely related to the word or phrase on the left. If necessary, use a dictionary to check the meaning of words you do not know.

		A	**B**
1.	a destination	(a place)	a time
2.	ingredients	(for a recipe)	for a suitcase
3.	a term	a direction	(a word)
4.	to require*	to give	(to need)
5.	a detail	a general idea	(a specific idea)
6.	catchy	(people like it)	people hate it
7.	to state	to believe	(to say)
8.	to allow	(to let)	to put
9.	to spread	(to move)	to stay
10.	trembling	(afraid, nervous)	sleepy, tired
11.	to take up	to move to a new area	(to occupy space)
12.	majority*	less than half	(more than half)
13.	an achievement*	something bad	(something good)
14.	to purchase*	(to buy)	to persuade
15.	entire	50 percent	(100 percent)

*Words that are part of the Academic Word List. See pages 275–276 for a complete list.

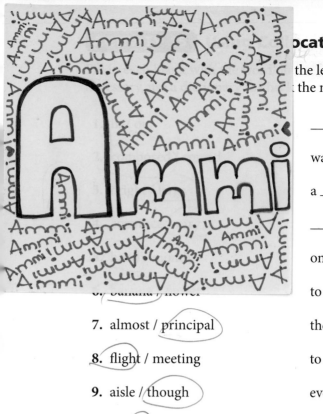

ocations

the left that most naturally completes the phrase on the right. If
the meaning of words you do not know.

_____ in _____ brief

water is ___composed___ of

a ___large___ gap

___vary___ considerably

on the other ___hand___

to peel a ___banana___

the ___principal___ reason for doing something

to board a ___flight___

even ___though___

differ ___in___

7. almost / (principal)

8. flight / meeting

9. aisle / (though)

10. (of / in)

Original Student Writing

ACTIVITY 16 **Original Writing Practice**

Write a simple paragraph. Follow these guidelines:

- Choose a general topic or look at the list on the next page for some ideas.
- Think of some specific aspect of that topic. Try to be as specific as you can. For example, you might choose "sports" as your first idea. Then you might choose "tennis." Finally you might choose "how to keep score in tennis."
- Write five to twelve related sentences.
- Include a topic sentence.
- Indent the first line.
- The last sentence should be a good concluding sentence.
- Give your paragraph a title.
- Use at least two of the vocabulary words or phrases presented in Activity 14 and Activity 15. Underline these words and phrases in your paragraph.

If you need ideas for words and phrases, see the Useful Vocabulary for Better Writing on pages 277–281.

Topic Ideas

Topic	Topic Sentence
Food	The easiest food to prepare is _____.
	The best meal I ever had was _____.
Color	Each color in my country's flag represents something special.
	Colors can affect the way you feel.
Sports	_____ (name a player) is an excellent _____ (name a sport) player.
	The rules for _____ (name a sport) are not (easy / difficult).
People	_____ has taught me many things about life.
	If I could meet anyone in history, I would like to meet _____.

Introduction to Peer Editing

Editing Your Writing

Good writers **proofread** their work and rewrite it several times. Think of the first draft of a paragraph as a first attempt.

Before you rewrite your paragraph or paper, it is also helpful to let someone else read it, offer comments, and ask questions to clarify your meaning. Many writers do not always see their own mistakes, but a reader can help you see where you need to make improvements.

In class, **peer editing** is an easy way to get opinions about your paper. In this method, other students (your peers) read your paper and make comments using a set of questions and guidelines. (See Peer Editing Sheets on NGL.Cengage.com/GW2.) You will read someone else's paper too. Peer editing can help you strengthen any areas in your paragraph that are weak or that appear confusing to the reader.

Suggestions for Peer Editing

1. Listen Carefully

In peer editing, you will receive some comments and suggestions from other students. It is important to listen carefully to comments about your writing. You may think that what you wrote is clear and accurate, but readers can often tell you what needs improvement. Remember that the comments are about the writing, not about you!

2. Make Helpful Comments

When you read your classmates' papers, choose your words and comments carefully so that you do not hurt their feelings. For example, instead of saying "This is bad grammar," or "I can't understand any of your ideas," make helpful comments, such as "You need to make sure that every sentence has a verb," or "What do you mean in this sentence?"

3. Study an Example of "Editing Your Writing"

Study the "Editing Your Writing" section of the *Brief Writer's Handbook with Activities* (pages 251–253). There are examples of edits and comments that a teacher made on a student's first draft and an example of the student's second draft.

4. Read, Read, Read!

It is important for you to understand why a piece of writing is good or is not good, and the best way to do this is to read, read, and read some more! The more writing styles you become familiar with, the better your writing can become, too.

Exchange papers from Activity 16 with a partner. Read your partner's paragraph. Then use Peer Editing Sheet 1 on NGL.Cengage.com/GW2 to help you comment on your partner's paragraph. There is a sample in the Appendix. Be sure to offer positive suggestions and comments that will help your partner write a better paragraph. Consider your partner's comments as you revise your own paragraph.

Additional Topics for Writing

Here are more ideas for writing. When you write, be sure to include the four features of a paragraph.

PHOTO
TOPIC : Look at the photo on pages 2–3. Write about something thrilling, such as a sport or a ride at an amusement park. When was it? Who did you go with? Was it scary or exciting? What happened?

TOPIC 2: Write about something easy to cook. What things do you need to make it? What are the steps you take to make it? How does it taste?

TOPIC 3: Write about a famous living person. What does this person do? Why is he/she famous?

TOPIC 4: Which is more difficult to learn: English or your language? What parts of the language do you find hard? Can you give suggestions for someone learning the language?

TOPIC 5: Write about your favorite season. What do you do during this season? How does it make you feel?

Timed Writing

How quickly can you write in English? There are many times when you must write quickly, such as on a test. It is important to feel comfortable during those times. Timed-writing practice can make you feel better about writing quickly in English.

1. Take out a piece of paper.

2. Read the writing prompt.

3. Brainstorm ideas for five minutes.

4. Write a short paragraph (six to ten sentences).

5. You have 25 minutes to write.

Describe the daily life of a police officer. Is being a police officer a good job? Is it easy? What kinds of things does a police officer do every day?

Developing Ideas for Writing a Paragraph

Lava flows out of the Pu'u O'o
vent of Kilauea Volcano in Hawaii.

Can you describe a scary event?

Brainstorming

How do writers find great topics for their paragraphs? One way to identify a really good topic for a paragraphs is **brainstorming**. Brainstorming is quickly writing down all the thoughts that come into your head. When you brainstorm, you do not think about whether an idea is good or bad or whether your writing is correct. You simply write to put your ideas on paper. This process is called brainstorming because it feels like there is a storm in your brain—a storm of ideas!

Imagine there is a fire in your hotel. What should you do? Study the ideas that one person might brainstorm.

Brainstorm your ideas!

ACTIVITY 1 **Brainstorming Practice**

Use this topic and situation to practice brainstorming. Work quickly. Do not worry about how good each idea is. For now, do not worry about correct spelling or grammar. Your immediate goal is to create a list of as many ideas as possible in just a few minutes.

Next Saturday is your grandmother's birthday. She is going to be 88 years old. What will you get for her? Make a list of five suitable birthday gifts for her.

1. _____

2. _____

3. _____

4. _____

5. _____

Compare your list to a classmate's list. Can you combine your best ideas with your classmate's best ideas? Sometimes it is helpful to work with other writers and share ideas. Remember that in brainstorming, there are no bad ideas. The purpose of brainstorming is to produce as many ideas as possible.

How Brainstorming Works

A good writer brainstorms about a topic by completing these two important steps:

- thinking about the topic

- writing down words and ideas

It is important to remember that the first step in writing a paragraph is not writing—it is **thinking**.

Brainstorming involves associating ideas because one idea can produce another. Some writers brainstorm in **lists**. Others **cluster** or connect their ideas in some other way. Consider this example of brainstorming for Example Paragraph 2, "An Easy Sandwich," on page 7. You can see that the writer wrote many ideas and crossed out some of them. There are several ideas that were not included in the final paragraph. In addition, a few ideas in the final paragraph are not in this list.

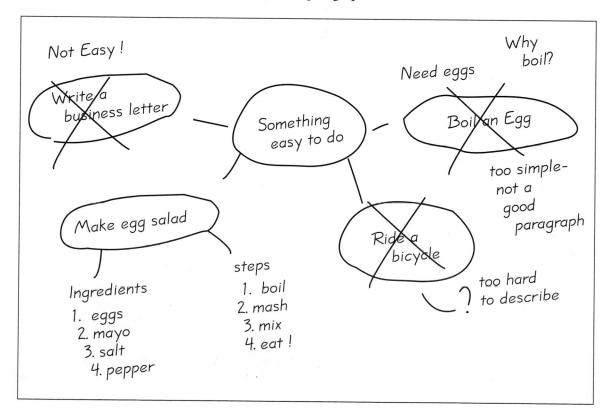

Follow these steps for each of the example topics:

1. Read the topic and brainstorm about the topic in the box. Make a list of ideas in English or use the diagram on page 35 as an example of how to connect ideas.

2. Circle the ideas that you think are the best ones to include in a paragraph.

3. Compare and discuss your ideas with a partner. When you compare your notes, be prepared to say why you want to keep some ideas and why you want to take out others. What information will be in the final paragraph?

Topic A: Terrifying Events

Brainstorm area:

Topic B: Important Inventions

Brainstorm area:

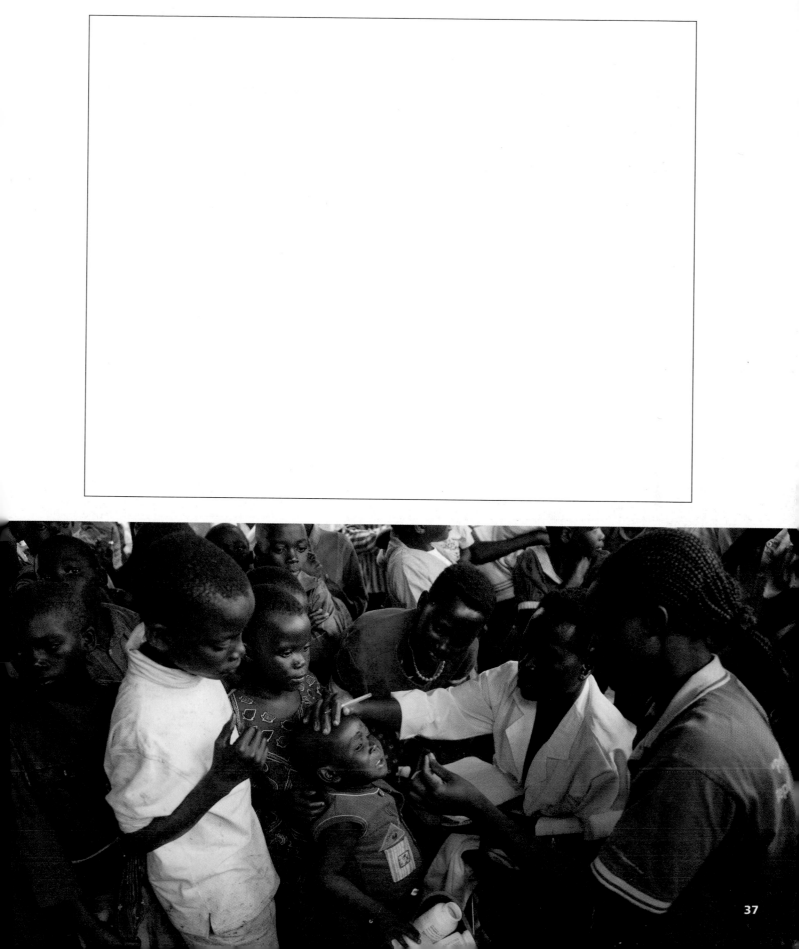

Topic C: Ideal Travel Destinations

Brainstorm area:

Choose an example paragraph that you read in Unit 1: "Chile and Brazil," "An Easy Sandwich," or "My First Flight." Brainstorm ideas that are related to the topic of one of these paragraphs. For example, if you choose "My First Flight," you might brainstorm about a frightening experience you had on an airplane or another experience that was scary.

- Which paragraph did you choose? _An Easy Sandwich._

- Why did you choose this paragraph? _is an easy topic_

Use the space below to brainstorm. If you prefer, work with another student who chose the same topic. Sometimes when you work with another writer, you get more ideas.

Brainstorm area:

Grammar for Writing

Subject-Verb Agreement

When writing, it is important that the verbs agree with the subjects. Notice the subject-verb agreement rules for the simple present.

Explanation	Examples
Use the base **form of the verb** for *I, you*, or plural words or pronouns.	I **prepare** you **prepare** we **prepare** they **prepare** my parents **prepare**
Use the **–s** form with third-person singular nouns or pronouns (*he, she, it*). The third person singular is formed by adding **–s** or **-es** to the end of the verb.	he **prepares** she **prepares** it **prepares** the cook **prepares** Bruno **cooks**
When writing, make sure the verb form matches the subject in number.	One boy **reads**. (singular) Two boy**s read**. (plural)
Remember to match the verb to the subject, not to other words in the sentence. Tip: Prepositional phrases start with prepositions (*at, for, by, with, without, in, of*) and include an object of the preposition (another noun). This is **not** the subject.	✗ The main **product** of Brazil and Colombia **are** coffee. ✓ The main **product** of Brazil and Colombia **is** coffee. ✗ The main **products** of Brazil **is** coffee and aluminum. ✓ The main **products** of Brazil **are** coffee and aluminum.
Tip: Collective nouns in North American English are often singular. Use the third person singular.	The United States **makes** many products. The team **wins** every game. The couple **works** in the city.
Tip: The noun after **there is** or **there are** is the subject of that sentence.	There **is a dictionary** on the table. There **are** three **reasons** for my decision.
Pronouns with **every-, some-,** or **any-** are always singular. Nouns with **each** or **every** are also singular.	**Everyone has** an accent of some kind. **Every** student **needs** a book and a workbook.
Spelling notes for the third person singular: When a verb ends in a consonant **+ y,** change the **-y** to **–i** and add **–es**. When a verb ends in **–ch, -sh, -ss, -x,** or **–zz,** add **–es**.	I try → he **tries** I watch → she **watches** I wash → he **washes** You miss → it **misses** They tax → the city **taxes** You buzz → it **buzzes**

Finding Subject-Verb Errors

Read the sentences. Find the 12 mistakes and correct them. If the sentence is correct, write C on the line.

1. _____R_____ Everybody lives near the coast because the interior is too dry.

2. _____C_____ A pair of scissors are necessary for this project.

3. _____ Laura carry her guitar from class to class every Thursday.

4. _____C_____ The main method of transportation in all of those tropical islands are the public bus system.

5. _____ The trees behind my house is dense.

6. _____ Earth revolve around the Sun.

7. _____ A pilot and a co-pilot flies the plane.

8. _____ The baby elephants at the zoo weighs just under 300 pounds.

9. _____ The coffee cups in the sink is still dirty.

10. _____ Professor Jones teachs Latin at 9 A.M. on Tuesdays and Thursdays.

11. _____ Most people in my town has a car.

12. _____ My family live near the ocean.

13. _____C_____ There are many interesting things to do in San Francisco.

14. _____ Every term the students tries new activities.

ACTIVITY 5 Practicing Subject-Verb Agreement

Underline the correct verb form in each sentence.

1. One reason I want to visit Asia (is, are) to see Japan.

2. In my opinion, the best tourist destinations in Japan (is, are) Tokyo and Kyoto.

3. Tokyo (is, are) a very modern city with many tall buildings.

4. In fact, the skyscrapers in Tokyo (is, are) some of the tallest buildings in the world.

5. However, the city skyline with these incredibly tall buildings (do, does) not look like the scenery in Kyoto at all.

6. Life in Kyoto (move, moves) at a much slower pace.

7. Kyoto (is, are) not only smaller but also much older.

8. In fact, Kyoto (was, were) the capital of Japan a long time ago.

9. Many of the traditional buildings still (exist, exists) there, so tourists can see them all over.

10. Life in these two places (is, are) quite different, and tourists (visit, visits) each city for very different reasons.

ACTIVITY 6 Correcting Subject-Verb Agreement Errors

Read this student paragraph. It contains seven errors in subject-verb agreement. Underline each error and write the correct form above it.

Example Paragraph 13

The Hard Work of a Teacher

Some people **may** think that Mimi Robertson has an easy job, but she really do not. Mimi is a kindergarten teacher at King Elementary School. She teaches 22 very young children. Mimi's class of kindergarten students begin at 8:30 a.m., but she does a lot before then. Every day she arrive at work just after 7:30 a.m. Mimi has to organize her supplies and prepare the room for her students. If one of the parents is in class that day to help, then Mimi have to explain the lesson plan to the parent before class. After the students arrive at 8:30, the class begins. The young students in her class keeps her **extremely** busy for the rest of the day. They play games and learn new things. However, there is always a few small problems. Mimi's young students does not always listen to her, and sometimes they fight or cry. Every now and then, one child **shouts**, but Mimi tries to be very patient with all of her students. After school, she **must** attend meetings and create new lessons. Mimi says she loves her job, but it really is **a great deal** of work.

may: possibly, might

extremely: very, to a high degree

to shout: to speak in a very loud voice, yell, scream

must: to be necessary, have to

a great deal (of): a large amount, a lot (*A lot* is used more in spoken English; *a great deal* sounds more formal and is more common in written English.)

Building Better Sentences: For further practice with the sentences and paragraphs in this unit, go to Practice 3 on pages 285–286 in Appendix 1.

Building Better Vocabulary

ACTIVITY 7 **Word Associations**

Circle the word or phrase that is most closely related to the word or phrase on the left. If necessary, use a dictionary to check the meaning of words you do not know.

	A	B
1. frightening	(afraid)	happy
2. to omit	(to forget)	to remember
3. interior	(inside)	outside
4. to revolve	to become	(to turn)
5. however	and	(but)
6. to shout	(loud voice)	soft voice
7. to share	to buy half	(to give half)
8. the purpose	(goal)	help
9. suddenly	perhaps	(surprise)
10. to create*	(to make)	to take
11. dense	a little in a big space	(a lot in a small space)
12. a skyscraper	(a type of building)	a type of weather
13. kindergarten	adults	(children)
14. suitable	bad idea	(good idea)
15. extremely	a little	(a lot)
16. a destination	a bus or a train	(a city or a town)

*Words that are part of the Academic Word List. See pages 275–276 for a complete list.

Fill in each blank with the word on the left that most naturally completes the phrase on the right. If necessary, use a dictionary to check the meaning of words you do not know.

1. in / on   depend __on__

2. cloud / room   a messy __room__

3. at / for   that book is not suitable __for__ a child

4. list / storm   make a __list__ of (something)

5. and / but   __and__ so on

6. in / out   cross __out__ an error

7. in / on   talking __on__ the phone

8. a page number / a long report   write down __a long report__

9. deal / must   a great __deal__ of (something)

10. expensive / price   extremely __expensive__

Original Student Writing

ACTIVITY 9 Writing a Paragraph from Brainstorming

Now it is your turn to write a simple paragraph. Follow these guidelines:

- Choose a topic from Activity 2 on pages 36–38.
- Use the ideas that you brainstormed about that topic to create sentences for your paragraph.
- Write five to twelve sentences.
- Include the four features of a good paragraph in this checklist from page 12.
    - ☐ 1. Does the paragraph have a topic sentence that states the main idea?
    - ☐ 2. Are all of the sentences in the paragraph about one topic?
    - ☐ 3. Is the first line of the paragraph indented?
    - ☐ 4. Is the last sentence a good concluding sentence?
- Give your paragraph a title.
- Be sure to proofread your paragraph for good sentences, vocabulary, and grammar.
- Be especially careful with subject-verb agreement.
- Use at least two of the vocabulary words or phrases presented in Activity 7 and Activity 8. Underline these words and phrases in your paragraph.

If you need ideas for words and phrases, see the Useful Vocabulary for Better Writing on page 277–281.

ACTIVITY 10 Peer Editing

Exchange papers from Activity 9 with a partner. Read your partner's paragraph. Then use Peer Editing Sheet 2 on NGL.Cengage.com/GW2 to help you comment on your partner's paragraph. Be sure to offer positive suggestions and comments that will help your partner improve his or her writing. Consider your partner's comments as you revise your own paragraph.

Additional Topics for Writing

Here are more ideas for writing. Start by brainstorming ideas. When you write, be sure to include the four features of a paragraph.

PHOTO
TOPIC: Look at the photo on pages 32–33. Write about something very scary that you experienced. What happened? When was it? How did you feel?

TOPIC 2: You and some friends want to go to an inexpensive restaurant. Where would you go? What would you order? Write about your night out together.

TOPIC 3: Write about and compare two things, people, or places. How are they similar? How are they different?

TOPIC 4: Write about ways that students can save money.

TOPIC 5: Write about three things that will be very different two years from now. Give specific examples with details.

Timed Writing

How quickly can you write in English? There are many times when you must write quickly, such as on a test. It is important to feel comfortable during those times. Timed-writing practice can make you feel better about writing quickly in English.

1. Take out a piece of paper.
2. Read the writing prompt.
3. Brainstorm ideas for five minutes.
4. Write a short paragraph (six to ten sentences).
5. You have 25 minutes to write.

In your opinion, is English easy or difficult to learn? Why do you think so? Give two or three strong reasons to support your opinion.

A woman is learning to
sky dive over São Paulo, Brazil.

OBJECTIVES To learn how to write a topic sentence
To use commas in sentences
To recognize and avoid sentence fragments, run-on sentences, and comma splices.

Can you write about learning something new?

The Topic Sentence

A **topic sentence** tells about the main idea of a paragraph. It is usually found at the beginning of a paragraph. In this unit, you will learn:

- the function of a topic sentence
- what a good topic sentence looks like
- how a good controlling idea guides the flow of the information in the paragraph

ACTIVITY 1 Studying a Topic Sentence in a Paragraph

Discuss the Preview Questions with your classmates. Then read the opinion paragraph and answer the questions that follow.

Preview Questions

1. How did you learn to drive a car? *may dad taught me*

2. Can you tell someone how to drive a car? Why is it difficult to explain? *yes, breaks you have to patient*

To Shift or Not to Shift

There are many **benefits** to driving a car with a **manual transmission**. First of all, a car with a manual transmission uses less gas than a car with an automatic transmission. A **typical economy car** can get **up to** 35 miles per gallon, but an automatic car averages 28. In addition to better gas mileage, a manual transmission allows the driver to start a car that has a low battery. With a foot on the **clutch**, the driver just needs to put the car in second **gear** and have someone push the car until it gains enough speed. The driver then **releases** the clutch quickly, and the car should start. Unfortunately, starting a car this way is impossible with an automatic transmission. Finally, people with manual transmissions say that they have much more control of their cars. For example, if the **brakes** suddenly stop working on this type of car, the driver can **shift** to a lower gear to slow the car down. In contrast, people who drive automatic transmission cars have to depend on the automatic system. If something **malfunctions**, drivers have no control of their vehicles. **While** automatic cars are more convenient, manual transmission cars certainly offer many more advantages.

a benefit: a good point; an advantage

manual: by hand

a transmission: a device in a vehicle that transfers power from the engine to the car to enable it to move

typical: usual, average

an economy car: an inexpensive car with good gas mileage

up to: not more than, that amount or lower

a clutch: the left pedal in a manual transmission car that allows shifting of gears

a gear: the part of a machine that has teeth or grooves around the edge and turns another part of the same machine

to release: to let go, allow to escape

a brake: the device that stops a vehicle

to shift: to change or move the gears in a car

to malfunction: to stop working, usually suddenly

while: although

Post-Reading

1. Which one of these ideas tells the purpose of this paragraph? Put a check mark ✓ next to the correct answer.

   _____ **a.** to talk about the different kinds of manual transmissions

   _____ **b.** to explain what a manual transmission is

   ___✓___ **c.** to tell why a manual transmission is better than an automatic transmission

   _____ **d.** to describe how a manual transmission interacts with the brakes in a vehicle

2. Underline the topic sentence in this paragraph.

3. A good paragraph has a very clear organization that you must learn. Underline the three sentences that introduce the three benefits of a manual transmission.

4. What is the purpose of the sentence that comes immediately after each of your three underlined sentences?

Show the benefits of driving a car with a manual trasmition.

5. The following expressions are important to the organization of the paragraph. What does each one mean? What is the purpose of each expression?

   a. first of all

   the first thing of all of it

   b. in addition to

   is to add somthing, also

   c. finally

   To end something last

ACTIVITY 2 **Recognizing Effective Topic Sentences**

What do you already know about topic sentences? Read each set of sentences. Write the general topic that the sentences share. Then put a check mark ✓ on the line next to the best topic sentence. Be prepared to explain your answers.

1. General Topic: ___winter___

   _____ Winter is a good season.

   _____ Winter weather is cold, and it snows.

   __✓__ The best season for kids is winter.

2. General Topic: ___soccer___

   __✓__ Soccer is popular for many reasons.

   _____ You need a leather ball to play soccer.

   _____ Soccer is a nice game.

3. General Topic: ___Los Angeles___

   _____ There are many people in Los Angeles.

   __✓__ People from many different cultures live in Los Angeles.

   _____ Los Angeles is a big city in California.

4. General Topic: _monolingual dictionaries_

_____ Monolingual dictionaries have only one language, but bilingual dictionaries have two languages.

__✓__ Many language students prefer bilingual dictionaries to monolingual dictionaries.

_____ Dictionaries that have two languages, such as French and English, are called bilingual dictionaries.

5. General Topic: _Perfumes_

__✓__ French perfumes are expensive for a number of reasons.

_____ My mother's perfume smells flowery.

_____ You can purchase perfumes in expensive blue crystal bottles.

6. General Topic: _A book or novel An American Education history_

_____ *An American Education* has 540 pages.

_____ A woman graduates in *An American Education*.

__✓__ *An American Education* is an excellent historical novel.

How did you decide which sentences were the best topic sentences? What were you looking for? Discuss your ideas with your classmates.

Features of a Good Topic Sentence

A good topic sentence has the following features:

1. It controls or guides the whole paragraph.

When you read the topic sentence, you know what to expect in the paragraph.

2. A good topic sentence is not a fact that everyone accepts as true.

For example, a bad topic sentence would be, "Libraries have books." The information in this sentence is true, but it is a fact and is not a good choice for a topic sentence.

3. A good topic sentence is specific.

"Tea is delicious" is not a good topic sentence because the information in the sentence is too general. The reader does not know what to expect in the paragraph. If you want to write a paragraph about tea, make your topic sentence more specific, such as "Green tea has many health benefits."

4. However, a good topic sentence is not too specific.

"This dictionary contains more than 42,000 words" limits the topic too much—there is nothing else for the writer to say.

5. A good topic sentence has a controlling idea.

It includes words or phrases that help guide the flow of ideas in the paragraph. The controlling idea focuses the content of the following sentences.

Controlling Ideas

Here are some example topic sentences with controlling ideas. The controlling ideas have been underlined.

1. <u>Many language students</u> prefer bilingual dictionaries to monolingual dictionaries.

   Explanation: The reader expects the paragraph to explain why this statement is true.

2. The <u>best season for kids</u> is winter.

   Explanation: The reader expects the paragraph to give reasons and examples of *why* winter is the best season for children.

3. People from <u>many different cultures</u> live in Los Angeles.

   Explanation: The reader expects the paragraph to include information about various groups of people *who* make up <u>the population of Los Angeles.</u>

4. Soccer is <u>popular for many reasons</u>.

   Explanation: The reader expects the paragraph to give a variety of information about soccer and *why* it is popular around the world.

Recognizing Controlling Ideas in Topic Sentences

Read the following topic sentences. The main idea for each sentence has been circled. Underline the controlling idea. Then explain what information you expect to find in the paragraph.

1. (The SAT Reasoning Test™) contains three distinct sections that deal with three important skills.

   Explanation: a list of 3 senctions and 3 skills.

2. (The shocking crash of a 747 jumbo jet) off the coast of New York baffled investigators.

   Explanation: The information about the crash..

3. (Crossword puzzles) are not only educational and fun but also addictive.

   Explanation: reason whys is Educational, Fun, and

4. Recent research has confirmed that (eating dark green, leafy vegetables,) such as broccoli and cabbage, may reduce the risk of some types of cancer.

   Explanation: reasons whys eating drak green vetablos redore the risk of mes

5. Although buying a house may seem appealing, (renting an apartment) has many advantages.

   Explanation: VERX

Building Better Sentences: For further practice with the sentences and paragraphs in this part of the unit, go to Practice 4 on page 286 in Appendix 1.

More Practice Recognizing Controlling Ideas

Read the three sentences in each item and then put a check mark ✓ next to the best topic sentence. Underline the controlling idea in that sentence. Be prepared to explain your selections.

1. _____ Most of the girls in the class get higher grades in English than the boys.

   _____ Research has shown that girls are better at languages than boys.

   _____ Many students like languages very much.

2. _____ Cats are better pets than goldfish for many reasons.

_____ Cats and goldfish are both animals.

_____ Cats cannot swim very well, but goldfish can.

3. _____ Yesterday I did not have lunch with my coworkers.

_____ Yesterday I went to work late.

_____ Yesterday was the worst day of my life.

4. _____ Some people call Paul Cézanne the father of modern art.

_____ Paul Cézanne, the father of modern art, made important contributions to the history of art.

_____ Paul Cézanne's art was not recognized until the end of his career, but he is often called the father of modern art.

5. _____ Many Canadians speak French, and some of them speak Chinese and Japanese.

_____ The current population of Canada is a reflection of the international background of its citizens and immigrants.

_____ A large number of new immigrants live in the western province of British Columbia, but not many of them speak German.

Adding Controlling Ideas to Create Better Topic Sentences

All of these topic sentences are too general. Rewrite each sentence and add a controlling idea. Compare your sentences with other students' sentences.

Example: Flowers are beautiful.

Flowers are the best gift to receive when you are feeling down.

OR

Only four kinds of flowers grow during the short summers in Alaska.

1. Cats are nice.

2. Paris is the capital of France.

3. The English alphabet has twenty-six letters.

4. Reading blogs is interesting.

5. Running is an enjoyable hobby.

ACTIVITY 6 **Studying a Topic Sentence in a Paragraph**

Answer these questions about how a topic sentence is related to the information in the body of the paragraph.

1. Copy the topic sentence from Paragraph 14 (page 49) here.

2. Underline the controlling idea(s) in that topic sentence.

3. Give at least three examples of how the controlling idea(s) in the topic sentence are directly connected to the information in the paragraph.

Read each paragraph on pages 56–60. Then write a good topic sentence that is connected to the information in the paragraph. Be sure to end each topic sentence with correct punctuation.

Example Paragraph 15

Reasons for Playing Instruments

_____

_____

_____

Some people choose to learn how to play a musical instrument because they want to have fun. They want to play it with their friends or maybe in a band. Another reason people play an instrument is that it is their hobby. They learned how to play it a long time ago, and now it is a way to occupy their time. Other people learn to play an instrument because it is part of their culture. Certain instruments are popular in one culture, **such as** the guitar in Spain or the **oud** in the Middle East. In some cases, however, people learn how to play an instrument because they think it will make them smarter. **A great deal of** research suggests that studying music can improve a person's brain function and intelligence. **In sum**, there is not just one main reason that people play a musical instrument.

such as: for example

the oud: a stringed instrument

a great deal of: much, a lot of

in sum: in conclusion

Differences Between Reptiles and Dinosaurs

_____

_____

_____

One is size. Most modern reptiles are small. Dinosaurs were much, much larger than any reptile that we have on earth today. Second, the legs of most reptiles today are on the sides of their body. However, dinosaurs' legs were on the bottom of their body. In this way, dinosaurs could stand up on their back legs. Third, today's reptiles use the environment to control their body temperature. In contrast, dinosaurs controlled their own body temperature. They did not depend on their surroundings. While reptiles and dinosaurs may seem very similar, they are actually quite different.

Example Paragraph 17

Reasons for Exercise

_____

_____

_____

First, your body will look better. Exercise is perfect for staying trim and healthy looking, and it does not have to take a long time. Second, you will actually have more energy. A person who exercises will have fewer problems walking up stairs or climbing hills. In addition, your heart will be healthier. A good, strong heart is necessary for a long, healthy life. Finally, exercise reduces stress and keeps your mind in shape. Therefore, if you want to improve your overall health, you should exercise three or four times each week to accomplish this goal.

Popular Popcorn

_____

_____

_____

It is one of the easiest foods to eat. You can eat it with your fingers, and it does not have to be served piping hot like some foods do. In addition, with only 20 calories per cup and almost no fat, it is both a filling and a heart-friendly snack. Furthermore, it can be an important **source** of natural fiber, a substance that is important in limiting certain types of cancer. Based on this information, can anyone be surprised that sales of popcorn are **soaring** in many countries?

a source: a place of origin

to soar: rise quickly

A Method for Learning New Words

_____

_____

_____

In this method, learners form their own sound association between the foreign language word they are trying to learn and any word in their native language. In the second stage, learners form an image link between the target word and the native language word. For example, a Japanese learner of English might look at the English word *hatchet* and connect it to the Japanese word *hachi*, which means "eight." In this case, the learner might remember that he can use a hatchet eight times to cut down a tree. For many language students, this particular method is effective in learning new vocabulary in a foreign language.

Building Better Sentences: For further practice with the sentences and paragraphs in this part of the unit, go to Practice 5 on page 287 in Appendix 1.

Grammar for Writing

Using Commas in Sentences

Commas are very important for clarity of meaning, but commas also represent the grammar of a sentence. Remember:

Explanation	Examples
A comma separates a list of three or more things.	I speak English, Spanish, and Japanese.
A comma separates two sentences when there is a combining word.	I speak three languages, **but** Adam speaks five.
A comma separates an introductory word or phrase from the rest of the sentence.	**First**, you will need to get a pencil.
A comma separates a dependent clause that comes at the beginning of a sentence.	**Because I speak three languages**, I can communicate with many people.
A comma separates an appositive from the rest of the sentence. (An appositive is a group of words that renames or explains the noun before it.)	Fiber, **a substance that is important in limiting certain types of cancer**, is found in popcorn.
A comma separates extra information that is provided in adjective clauses.	*The History of Korea*, **which is on the teacher's desk**, is the book for the course.

For more information and examples, review the section on "Commas" in the *Brief Writers Handbook with Activities*, pages 258–260.

Insert commas in these sentences where necessary. Be prepared to explain your choices. Some sentences are correct with no commas.

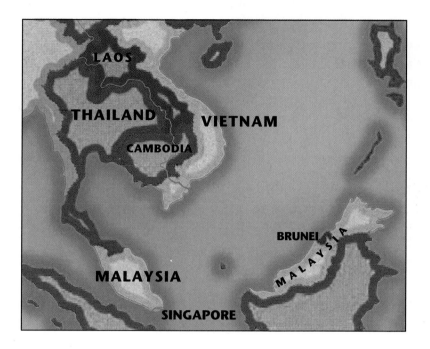

Example Paragraph 20

Malaysia and Thailand

Because Malaysia and Thailand are located next to each other we might conclude that these two nations share many similarities. To a certain extent this conclusion is true. For example both countries have temperate climates throughout the year. Thailand's economy is growing and so is Malaysia's. In addition Malaysia has many miles of beautiful beaches that attract tourists and Thailand does too. However there are also several important differences. Malaysians and Thais speak completely different languages. The population of Malaysia is about 29 million but the population of Thailand is about 69 million. Thailand has a national king but Malaysia does not. Finally Malaysia was a British colony but Thailand was never a British colony. **Thus** the fact that two countries are near each other does not always mean they are similar.

thus: therefore, for this reason

Grammar for Writing

Avoiding Three Common Sentence Errors

Three common mistakes in writing are **sentence fragments, run-on sentences, and comma splices.** These mistakes can prevent the reader from understanding the writer's message.

Explanation	Examples
A **sentence fragment** is not a complete sentence. It is usually missing either a subject or a verb, or it is a dependent clause. A dependent clause is never a complete sentence. To correct a sentence fragment: • add a subject or verb, or • combine two clauses	✗ I went to Italy last summer. <u>Was a wonderful trip.</u> ✓ I went to Italy last summer. **It** was a wonderful trip. *(add a subject)* ✗ Only 120 students majored in <u>art. Because</u> they are worried about job opportunities. ✓ Only 120 students majored in art **because** they are worried about job opportunities. *(combine two clauses)*
A **run-on sentence** is two sentences incorrectly joined without a comma or a coordinating conjunction (*and, or, but, so, yet, nor, for*). To correct a run-on sentence: • add a comma and a connecting word, or • separate the sentences into two with a period	✗ I went to Italy and saw <u>Rome I</u> didn't get to see Milan. ✓ I went to Italy and saw Rome**, but** I didn't get to see Milan. *(add comma and connecting word)* ✓ I went to Italy and saw Rome. I didn't get to see Milan. *(separate into two sentences)*
A **comma splice** occurs when two or more sentences or independent clauses are connected with a comma. To correct a comma splice: • add a connecting word after the comma, • create two sentences from the one, or • combine the most important words from the two sentences into one sentence and add a subordinating conjunction (*because, since, although*)	✗ I went to Italy last <u>summer, it</u> was a wonderful trip. ✓ I went to Italy last summer, **and** it was a wonderful trip. *(add connecting word)* ✓ I went to Italy last summer. It was a wonderful trip. *(create two sentences)* ✗ Only 120 students majored in <u>art, because</u> they are worried about job opportunities. ✓ Only 120 students majored in art **because** they are worried about job opportunities. ✓ **Because** they are worried about job opportunities, only 120 students majored in art. *(add a subordinating conjunction)*

Read each group of words. If it is a complete sentence, write *C* on the line. If it is a sentence fragment, write *SF* on the line. Then write a correct sentence. More than one correction may be possible.

1. __SF__ One of the most common reasons that people make a decision to become a vegetarian.

   One of the most common reasons that people make a decision to become a

   vegetarian is to improve their health.

2. __SF__ Because the wind and rain were so incredibly strong between noon and 4 p.m. yesterday.

   We could go, Because

   _____

3. __C__ Although the price of gasoline is extremely high, people just complain and pay the high prices.

   _____

   _____

4. _____ In order to cash a check at a bank where you do not have an account and no one there knows you.

   _____

   _____

5. __C__ Of course the main ingredient that you have to have in order to make chicken soup is chicken.

   _____

   _____

6. _____ For some teachers, a sentence fragment is a very serious type of mistake because it shows a lack of understanding of what a sentence is.

   The economic

7. __SF__ Although the economic forecast for the housing market does not contain any especially bright news for those who wish to buy a house in the near future.

   _____

   _____

8. __C__ When the vice-president was sworn in as the new number two person in the entire country, her husband and her children as well as her grandchildren attended the ceremony.

   _____

   _____

ACTIVITY 10 **Correcting Sentence Fragments, Run-On Sentences, and Comma Splices**

Read each sentence or set of sentences. If it is correct, write *C* on the line. If there is an error, circle it and indicate the type of error by writing SF for a sentence fragment, *RO* for run-on sentence, or *CS* for a comma splice. Then write the correct sentence(s). More than one correction may be possible.

1. ___CS___ A whale is one of the largest animals on the (planet, few) people have seen one in person.

   A whale is one of the largest animals on the planet. Few people have seen one in person.

   OR

   Although the whale is one of the largest animals on the planet, few people have seen one in person.

2. _____ Yesterday's weather caused problems for many travelers. Most of the flights were canceled. Due to the torrential rains and high winds.

   _____

   _____

   _____

3. ___CS___ Computer programs can help students learn a foreign language, many students use the language programs in the computer center.

   _____

   _____

   _____

4. _C_ It was definitely a nervous time for many people. When we had the economic crisis, prices and unemployment soared. The government did everything possible to make sure that people did not panic.

_____

_____

5. _CS_ *Dancing with the Stars* is an internationally known television show, the dancing is very exciting.

_____

_____

6. _SF_ This magazine won several awards last year. For the content and the style of its stories. The last issue had two superb short stories that were written by distinguished authors.

_____

_____

7. _SF_ Lázaro Cárdenas was the president of Mexico from 1934 to 1940. His original goal was to become a teacher, but the political situation in Mexico at that time caused him to change his mind.

_____

_____

8. _SF_ Despite all of the extremely depressing news that we recently heard from that part of the world, the people remain optimistic.

_____

_____

Building Better Sentences: For further practice with the sentences and paragraphs in this part of the unit, go to Practice 6 on pages 287–288 in Appendix 1.

Building Better Vocabulary

ACTIVITY 11 Word Associations

Circle the word or phrase that is most closely related to the word or phrase on the left. If necessary, use a dictionary to check the meaning of words you do not know.

		A	B
1.	a reptile	(animal)	disease
2.	utensils	people	(things)
3.	distinguished	(known)	secret
4.	brakes	you use them to start a car	(you use them to stop a car)
5.	to reduce	(to become smaller)	to become bigger
6.	an axle	(wheels)	windows
7.	a device*	a person	(a thing)
8.	to purchase*	(to buy)	to sell
9.	to baffle	(to confuse)	to decide
10.	up to six things	(four or five things)	seven or eight things
11.	while	after	(although)
12.	an appealing idea	people hate it	(people like it)
13.	a risk	(a danger)	a product
14.	a snack	a kind of animal	(a kind of food)
15.	the source*	(where something came from)	why someone did something

*Words that are part of the Academic Word List. See pages 275–276 for a complete list.

ACTIVITY 12 Using Collocations

Fill in each blank with the word on the left that most naturally completes the phrase on the right. If necessary, use a dictionary to check the meaning of words you do not know.

1.	by / with	handicrafts are made _____by_____ hand
2.	car / fiber	an economy _____car_____
3.	from / with	interact _____with_____

4. first / next   _____First_____ of all

5. bilingual / soaring   _____soaring_____ prices

6. as / for   vegetables such _____as_____ onions

7. than / that   one thing is easier _____than_____ another

8. by / of   one thing is a reflection _____of_____ another thing

9. in / on   depend _____on_____ a good friend

10. filling / trembling   a _____filling_____ meal

Original Student Writing

ACTIVITY 13 **Brainstorming Ideas for a Paragraph**

Choose one of the general topics below. Brainstorm your ideas about it in the space provided. When you have finished, circle the ideas that you think are best to include in a paragraph.

Topics:

1. animal communication
2. international flights
3. pollution
4. smart phones

Brainstorming area:

ACTIVITY 14 **Original Writing Practice**

Use your brainstorming notes from Activity 13 on page 67 to write a paragraph.

- Make sure that your paragraph has the four features explained on page 12.
- Use at least two of the vocabulary words or phrases presented in Activity 11 and Activity 12. Underline the words and phrases in your paragraph.

If you need ideas for words and phrases, see the Useful Vocabulary for Better Writing on pages 277–281.

ACTIVITY 15 **Peer Editing**

Exchange papers from Activity 14 with a partner. Read your partner's paragraph. Then use Peer Editing Sheet 3 on page NGL.Cengage.com/GW2 to help you comment on your partner's paragraph. Be sure to offer positive suggestions and comments that will help your partner improve his or her writing. Consider your partner's comments as you revise your own paragraph.

Additional Topics for Writing

Here are more ideas for writing. Start by brainstorming. When you write your paragraph, be sure to include the four features of a paragraph.

PHOTO
TOPIC: Look at the photo on pages 46–47. Write about learning something new. What would you learn? Would you learn about it inside or outside? What would you do with the new information or skill?

TOPIC 2: Write about your daily routine. What do you do and when? How many things do you do in a day? What is the best part of your day or week?

TOPIC 3: Write about a famous person you would like to meet. What has this person done that is interesting to you? What would you talk about? What would you hope to learn from the experience?

TOPIC 4: Write about two vacation destinations. Which is better? Compare the sights. What is similar, and what is different? What are some activities you can do while in each of these places?

TOPIC 5: Write about your favorite relative. Who is this person? What qualities make this person special? How does this person make others feel?

Timed Writing

How quickly can you write in English? There are many times when you must write quickly, such as on a test. It is important to feel comfortable during those times. Timed-writing practice can make you feel better about writing quickly in English.

1. Take out a piece of paper.

2. Read the writing prompt.

3. Brainstorm ideas for five minutes.

4. Write a short paragraph (six to ten sentences).

5. You have 25 minutes to write your paragraph.

In your opinion, why do so many people want to learn English? Give a few strong examples to support your answer.

Supporting and Concluding Sentences

A cable car is going toward the
top of Sugarloaf Mountain in
Rio de Janeiro, Brazil

To learn how to write supporting sentences
To learn how to write concluding sentences
To substitute pronouns for key nouns

**Can you write about a place
to visit in your city?**

Supporting Sentences

Supporting sentences give information that explains and expands the topic of the paragraph. They answer questions—*who? what? where? when? why?* and *how?*—and give details. Good writers think of these questions when they write supporting sentences for the topic sentence.

ACTIVITY 1 **Predicting Paragraph Content from the Controlling Idea**

Read each topic sentence. Circle the main idea. Underline the controlling idea. Then predict the kind of information you will find in the paragraph.

1. New York and Boston attract millions of tourists, but I think one of the best cities to visit on the east coast of the United States is Washington, D.C.

   What kind of information do you think is in this paragraph?

   _____

   _____

   _____

   _____

2. One of the people that I most admire is my great-grandmother Carla.

   What kind of information do you think is in this paragraph?

   _____

   _____

   _____

   _____

3. The Grand Palace is one of the most popular tourist destinations in Thailand.

   What kind of information do you think is in this paragraph?

   _____

   _____

   _____

   _____

As you can see, the topic sentences are all very different. As a result, the supporting sentences that you write will depend on your topic sentence.

ACTIVITY 2 **Reading Example Supporting Sentences**

Read the paragraphs on pages 73–75. Notice how the supporting sentences tell you more about the topic sentence. Compare what you wrote in Activity 1 to the information in each paragraph. How well did you predict the content?

Example Paragraph 21

A Great Tourist Destination

New York and Boston attract millions of tourists, but I think one of the best cities to visit on the east coast of the United States is Washington, D.C. It has some of the most interesting **landmarks** and tourist **spots** in the country. There are many monuments to visit, such as the Lincoln Memorial, the Jefferson Memorial, and the Washington Monument, which is the tallest building in Washington. For more excitement, the area called Georgetown in northwest Washington is famous for its shopping and restaurants. Finally, there is the White House tour. On this tour, the guide **leads** visitors as they walk through many of the rooms in the White House and **view** the home of the president of the United States. Although Washington, D.C., does not have the large number of visitors that New York or Boston does, I think this city is one of the best destinations for tourists.

a landmark: a historical building, a well-known location

a spot: a place, a location

to lead: to show the way, organize

to view: to see, look at

Example Paragraph 22

An Immigrant in the Family

One of the people that I admire the most is my great-grandmother Carla. She came to the United States from Italy in 1911 as a young woman on a large ship. She had little money and no **property**. Soon after landing at Ellis Island in New York, she began working as a **seamstress** in Brooklyn. She met and married my great-grandfather not long after that. They immediately began their large family. Great-grandma Carla had eight children—five boys and three girls. In addition to taking care of **such** a large family in a new country, my great-grandmother survived **discrimination** as an **immigrant**, two world wars, the Great Depression, and a long list of illnesses. However, she rarely **complained**, and she was very happy with her new life in America. Whenever I think of my great-grandma Carla, I am always filled with **admiration** for her.

the property: land or buildings that a person owns

a seamstress: a woman who sews for a living

such: to a great degree, very

the discrimination: unfair treatment, especially because of race, age, or gender

an immigrant: a person who comes to live in a new country

to complain: to express unhappiness or dissatisfaction about something

admiration: a feeling of approval or pleasure for someone

The Grand Palace in Bangkok

The Grand Palace is one of the most popular tourist destinations in Thailand. The **construction** of the palace began in 1782, and the royal family lived there until 1925. The palace area **consists of** over two million square feet, and the wall that surrounds the Grand Palace is more than 6,000 feet long. This huge area includes countless buildings, gardens, and special rooms. The public cannot visit all of these areas, however, because some areas are still used for official events. The palace includes some examples of European influence on the design, such as the Greek columns and the French windows. It is certainly easy to understand why so many tourists visit the Grand Palace each year.

the construction: the act of building something

to consist of: contain, include

Kinds of Supporting Sentences

Good supporting sentences have different goals. Writers vary them to:

- **explain:**   The family moved from the village to the capital for economic reasons.
- **describe:**   She lived in a lovely three-story castle surrounded by a forest.
- **give reasons:** Lukas finally quit his job because of the stressful working conditions.
- **give facts:**   More than ten percent of the university's student population is international.
- **give examples:** Oranges and grapefruits grow in California.
- **define:**   Many tourists visit Bangkok, which is the capital and largest city in Thailand.

ACTIVITY 3 **Matching Supporting and Topic Sentences**

Read the two topic sentences below. Then read the list of supporting sentences. Match each supporting sentence with the corresponding topic sentence by writing the correct topic sentence number on the line beside the supporting sentences. Notice that each sentence is labeled in parentheses with the kind of supporting sentence that it is.

Topic sentences

TS 1: Low-fat diets are an excellent way to stay healthy and trim.

TS 2: High-protein diets are favored by athletes and competitors.

Supporting sentences

a. __2__ These foods help build muscles and increase energy. (fact)

b. __1__ They are preferred by the general public because they help with weight reduction. (reason)

c. __1__ Low-fat diets are recommended by most physicians. (fact)

d. __2__ Many athletes eat high-protein foods, such as meat, beans, and nuts. (example)

e. __1__ Low-fat foods include fruits, vegetables, and pasta. (example)

f. __1__ Because they are easy to find in stores, low-fat foods are convenient. (reason)

g. __2__ Athletes generally eat high-protein diets to give them more energy. (reason)

h. __1__ Crispy steamed vegetables and grilled fish and chicken are all tasty parts of a low-fat, heart-friendly diet. (description)

ACTIVITY 4 **Asking Questions about Topic Sentences**

Read each topic sentence. What information would you expect the writer to include in the paragraph? Write a question that the supporting sentences should answer. Use a *who? what? where? when? why?* or *how?* question.

> In 2008, smoking was banned in all public facilities.
> ___Why was smoking banned?___

1. Texas is home to several kinds of poisonous snakes.

what kind

2. Classrooms without windows have negative effects on students.

_____

3. Computer technology will one day eliminate the use of libraries.

_____

4. Quebec City is a wonderful place to raise children.

_____

5. I will never forget the day I got married.

_____

Building Better Sentences: For further practice with the sentences and paragraphs in this part of the unit, go to Practice 7 on pages 288–289 in Appendix 1.

ACTIVITY 5 **Brainstorming Topic Sentences**

For each of the general topics in the left column, brainstorm some ideas in the space provided. Then write a topic sentence with a controlling idea in the right column. Underline the controlling ideas.

Brainstorming Topic	Topic Sentence with Controlling Idea
1. vacation • types (summer; honeymoon) • 5 common destinations (national parks, Caribbean islands) • memories (Why was it special?)	I will <u>never forget</u> my summer vacation.
2. mathematics	
3. a best friend	

4. a meal you ate at a restaurant	
5. a (specific) sport	

Asking for More Information

Choose two of your topic sentences from Activity 5 and write them below. Then write four questions about each topic. Remember to use *who? what? where? when? why?* or *how?* questions. If you cannot think of four questions, brainstorm some ideas with a classmate.

1. Topic Sentence: _____ I will never forget my summer vacation. _____

    a. _____ Why was this vacation so memorable? _____

    b. _____ Where did you go? _____

    c. _____ What did you do? _____

    d. _____ How old were you at that time? _____

2. Topic Sentence: _____

    a. _____

    b. _____

    c. _____

    d. _____

3. Topic Sentence: _____

    a. _____

    b. _____

    c. _____

    d. _____

Unrelated Information

Sometimes writers give information that is not closely related to the topic. When this happens, the paragraph does not read smoothly, and the reader might get confused about the writer's message. It is necessary that each sentence in a paragraph be connected to the controlling idea or ideas in the topic sentence of the paragraph.

ACTIVITY 7 Identifying the Unrelated Sentence

Read the paragraphs on pages 79–81. In each paragraph, underline the one sentence that does not belong because it is not connected closely with the supporting ideas in the topic sentence.

Example Paragraph 24

My Evaluation of Dining at Fresh Market

The menu at Fresh Market, one of the newest restaurants in downtown Springfield, consists of only five main dishes that are simple but very delicious. My number one dish there is pasta with fresh vegetables. The pasta is cooked just right, and the vegetables include broccoli, onions, tomatoes, and corn. My second favorite main dish is the spicy chicken and brown rice soup. The chicken is a little hot for some people's tastes, but many people really like the fact that you get brown rice instead of the usual bland white rice. The other main dishes are fried chicken with curry potatoes, Greek salad with grilled shrimp, and fried fish with vinegar chips. All three of these use the freshest of ingredients and taste great. This paragraph will not include any information about the beverages at this restaurant. If you eat a meal at Fresh Market, I am sure you will enjoy it tremendously.

Example Paragraph 25

Counting the Continents

The number of continents should be a simple fact, but the number you identify depends on where you live. In the United States, students learn that there are seven continents. These seven are North America, South America, Europe, Africa, Asia, Australia, and Antarctica. In Europe, however, students learn that there are six continents. They learn that North America and South America are one continent, which they call the Americas. Panama is the southern end of North America, but it used to be part of Colombia, which is in South America. In some places, Europe and Asia are combined into one continent called Eurasia. In other places, Antarctica is not considered a continent. It is very interesting that different cultures clearly disagree on the definition of a continent and therefore the number of continents on our earth.

Traveling between Rome and Paris

There are three good options for traveling between Rome and Paris. The fastest way is by plane. However, flying between these two cities can be a little expensive unless you can find a discounted airline ticket. The second way is by train, which is very popular with many tourists. In fact, Rome and Paris are visited each year by millions of students from all over. The train fare is not so expensive and the service is very good, but the overnight trip takes about 14 hours. Finally, many people take a bus. The bus is the cheapest of the three options, but it takes up to 22 hours, which means it takes the most time. If you research each of these three travel options, you will find the best way for you to travel between Rome and Paris.

Read each paragraph on pages 82–84.

1. For each of the underlined, numbered sentences, write *good supporting sentence* or *unrelated sentence* on the corresponding lines below the paragraph. (One sentence in each paragraph is unrelated to the topic.)

2. Write a reason for each choice.

Remember: All the supporting sentences must be related to the topic sentence. The first paragraph has been done for you.

Example Paragraph 27

Strict Parents

Fortunately, my parents were very strict with me when I was a child. I think that they were protective because I was an only child. However, at that time, it felt like I was in prison. I had to come straight home after school and immediately do my homework. **1** After I finished my homework, I was allowed to watch only one hour of television. While my friends were playing video games or watching cartoons, I was usually doing chores around the house to help my mother. **2** This included doing some of the laundry and ironing, mowing the lawn, and helping to prepare dinner. **3** My father was an architect, and my mother was a housewife. Looking back, I am not sorry that my parents were strict with me because I think it was the best way to bring up a child.

1. *good supporting sentence* — It is an example of why the writer felt he or she was in prison.

2. *good supporting sentence* — It is a list of the chores the writer had to do around the house.

3. *unrelated sentence* — The writer's parents' occupations are not related to how the writer was treated. There is no relationship between being an architect and being a strict parent.

Underwater Adventure

Snorkeling can be one of the most amazing adventures you can ever take part in. **1** <u>Floating on the water and watching the fish swim below you is a unique experience</u>. It is normal to be nervous in the beginning, but once you are in the water, the anxiety goes away as you slowly notice the new world around you. Coral reefs are the best places to snorkel because hundreds, sometimes thousands, of fish and other sea creatures live among the coral. **2** <u>Depending on where you snorkel, you can see tiny squids, turtles, sea cucumbers, lobsters, and many other animals</u>. **3** <u>I saw a shark the last time I was snorkeling, and it really scared me.</u> It is truly a beautiful sight, one that you can hardly believe is happening. When you are underwater, the world you know is blocked out, and the silence makes the overall experience more magical. If you want to have one of the most beautiful experiences that anyone can ever have, you should try snorkeling for a day.

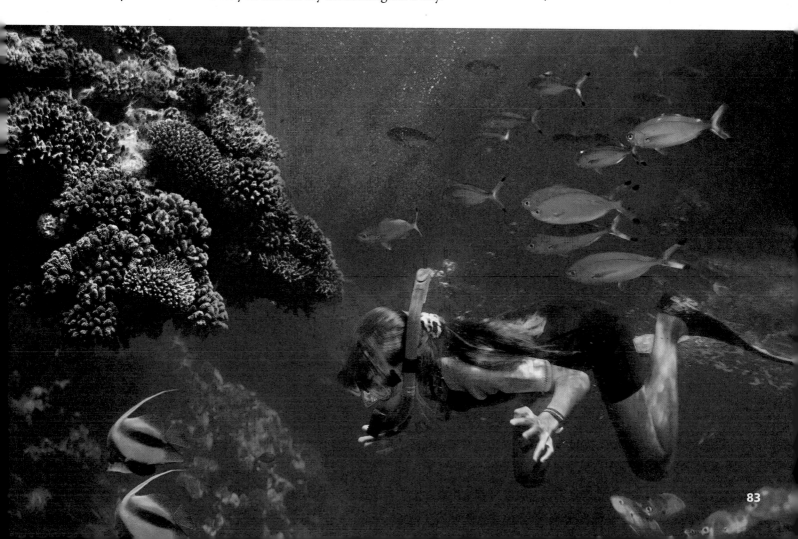

1. _____ _____
   _____
2. _____ _____
   _____
3. _____ _____
   _____

Sweet Dreams

When people have a hard time falling asleep at night, there are three things that they can do to relax before going to sleep. **1** <u>One of the most pleasant ways to relax is to imagine a beautiful and peaceful place.</u> This requires a creative mind, but it is very effective. Another common method is to practice deep-breathing exercises. These rhythmic exercises are good for getting rid of the tension that causes people to stay awake. **2** <u>A third method is to listen to relaxing music, especially soft music.</u> **3** <u>Soft music is also popular because it helps students study better.</u> Some people have developed unique ways to help them fall asleep, but these three methods are extremely effective for the majority of people with sleep problems.

1. _____ _____
   _____
2. _____ _____
   _____
3. _____ _____
   _____

Grammar for Writing

Using Pronouns in Place of Key Nouns

Because a paragraph is about one topic, writers often repeat key nouns from the topic sentence in their supporting sentences. However, too much repetition of these same nouns can sound awkward. You can avoid repeating key nouns by replacing them with **pronouns** after the nouns are first introduced.

Explanation	Examples
Pronouns take the place of a person, place, or thing: Carla → She Washington → It Giraffes → They Replace nouns with pronouns to avoid repetition.	One of the best cities to visit on the east coast of the United States is **Washington, D.C. It** has some of the most interesting landmarks and tourist spots in the country. One of the people that I most admire is **my great-grandmother Carla. She** came to the United States from Italy in 1911 as a young woman on a large ship.
Remember to be consistent. If you use *they* at the beginning of a paragraph, do not switch to *it*. The underlined words are incorrect in the example.	**Giraffes** are among the most interesting of all the animals that live in Africa. **They** are easily recognized by **their** special features. **They** have long necks and long legs, but its neck is longer than its legs. It usually lives in very dry areas.

ACTIVITY 9   Identifying Key Nouns and Pronouns

Read the following sentences. Write the correct pronoun in each blank. Use *it, they,* or *we*. Then underline the key noun that the pronoun refers to.

1. <u>Tennis rackets</u> have changed tremendously in the last ten years. _____They_____ used to be small and heavy, but that is no longer true.

2. Soccer is by far the most widely played sport in the world. _____ is played professionally on nearly every continent.

3. I will never forget my childhood friends Carlos and Juan and what _____ taught me.

4. Not only is text messaging fast, but _____ is also an interesting way to practice English.

5. A bad thing happened to my classmates and me at school yesterday. _____ were late coming to class, so the teacher gave us an extra homework assignment.

6. If you travel to Budapest, Hungary, you will fall in love with the Danube River. _____ separates the city into two parts—Buda and Pest.

Writer's Note

Staying on Track

As you write a paragraph, always look back at your topic sentence. Do not include any information that is unrelated to the topic sentence. It is very easy to lose track of the main idea if you do not refer to the topic sentence from time to time.

Concluding Sentences

The **concluding sentence** is the last sentence of the paragraph. It concludes, or wraps up, a paragraph. It lets the reader know that you have finished talking about the idea introduced by the topic sentence.

A concluding sentence often has one of these four important purposes:

1. It restates the main idea.
2. It offers a suggestion.

3. It gives an opinion.
4. It makes a prediction.

Restates the Main Idea

Perhaps the easiest concluding sentence to write is one that simply restates the main idea or summarizes the main points of the paragraph. The following transitional words and phrases are commonly used at the beginning of a concluding sentence:

as a result	overall	for this reason
certainly	because of this	surely
in conclusion	therefore	for these reasons
clearly	thus	in brief

Examples:

Paragraph 4, page 13

Topic Sentence	At some point, most parents have to decide whether or not to allow their children to have pets.
Concluding Sentence	In brief, although many children want a pet, parents are divided on this issue for a number of important reasons.

Explanation: The information in this concluding sentence is very similar to the topic sentence. In addition, the concluding sentence includes the phrase "a number of important reasons" because the paragraph includes several reasons for allowing or not allowing children to have pets.

Paragraph 5, page 15

Topic Sentence	eBook readers are excellent devices for students.
Concluding Sentence	It is clear that eBook readers have made students' lives much easier.

Explanation: This concluding sentence also restates the idea of the topic sentence. The examples in the paragraph show how eBook readers simplify students' lives, and the concluding sentence emphasizes this fact.

Offers a Suggestion, Gives an Opinion, or Makes a Prediction

A concluding statement can offer a suggestion, give an opinion, or make a prediction. Sometimes a concluding statement does a combination of these three options.

Examples:

Paragraph 28, page 83

Topic Sentence	Snorkeling can be one of the most amazing adventures you can ever take part in.
Concluding Sentence	If you want to have one of the most beautiful experiences that anyone can ever have, you should try snorkeling for a day.

Explanation: This topic sentence introduces snorkeling as an amazing adventure, and the concluding sentence offers a **suggestion** that the reader should try snorkeling.

Paragraph 27, page 82

Topic Sentence	Fortunately, my parents were very strict with me when I was a child.
Concluding Sentence	Looking back, I am not sorry that my parents were strict with me because I think it was the best way to bring up a child.

Explanation: This topic sentence explains that the writer's parents were very strict. In the concluding sentence, the writer gives his **opinion** that being a strict parent is the best way to raise a child.

Paragraph 24, page 79

Topic Sentence	The menu at Fresh Market, one of the newest restaurants in downtown Springfield, consists of only five main dishes that are simple but very delicious.
Concluding Sentence	If you eat a meal at Fresh Market, I am sure you will enjoy it tremendously.

Explanation: This topic sentence informs us that the menu at Fresh Market has only five dishes and they are very delicious. The concluding sentence makes a **prediction** that you will enjoy this place very much if you eat there.

ACTIVITY 10 Analyzing Concluding Sentences

Go back to the Example Paragraphs listed. Write the concluding sentence from these paragraphs and then check its purpose.

1. Example Paragraph 21 (page 73)

   Topic: Washington, D.C.

   _____

   _____

   What does the concluding statement do?

   ❏ restates the main idea   ❏ offers a suggestion   ❏ gives an opinion   ❏ makes a prediction

2. Example Paragraph 17 (page 58)

   Topic: Exercise

   _____

   _____

   What does the concluding statement do?

   ❏ restates the main idea   ❏ offers a suggestion   ❏ gives an opinion   ❏ makes a prediction

3. Example Paragraph 2 (page 7)

   Topic: Egg Salad

   _____

   _____

   What does the concluding statement do?

   ❏ restates the main idea   ❏ offers a suggestion   ❏ gives an opinion   ❏ makes a prediction

4. Example Paragraph 3 (page 10)

Topic: My First Flight

_____

_____

What does the concluding statement do?

❏ restates the main idea   ❏ offers a suggestion   ❏ gives an opinion   ❏ makes a prediction

ACTIVITY 11 **Analyzing Paragraphs**

Read each paragraph on pages 88–90 and:

1. Underline the topic sentence and write TS above it.

2. Circle any sentence that is not a good supporting sentence based on the controlling idea in the topic sentence.

3. Write a concluding sentence on the lines provided.

Example Paragraph 30

College Adjustments

When I first started going to college, I was surprised at all the studying that was required. I had to **adjust** my study habits because in high school I hardly ever studied, **yet** my grades were still fairly good. At the university, it seemed that all my professors thought their class was the most important class. Each professor gave me a **tremendous** amount of homework every night. As a result, my free time became very limited. Nights out with friends and time spent watching TV were **replaced** with reading assignments, group projects, learning activities, and research. My university classes kept me so busy that I could only go out on Saturday nights. This kind of schedule was a big change from high school, where I **used to** play sports, have fun, and go out **every other** night.

_____

_____

_____

to adjust: to change a little

yet: but, however

tremendous: great; huge

to replace: to substitute one thing for another

used to + verb: to do an action many times in the past but no longer

every other: alternating

Different Names for the Same Kind of Storm

When bad weather, thunder, and strong winds mix, the result is a dangerous storm, but the name for that storm differs according to where the storm occurs. When a storm forms in the Atlantic or eastern Pacific Ocean, it is called a hurricane. This type of storm can be dangerous to people living in the United States, Mexico, Central America, or the Caribbean islands. When a large storm begins in the southern Pacific Ocean, this same type of storm is called a cyclone. Cyclones are less common **due to** the colder temperature of the water there. Finally, if this same storm begins in the western Pacific Ocean, it is referred to as a typhoon. Typhoons are usually stronger than hurricanes, and they **endanger** people living in areas such as Japan, Guam, or the Philippines.

_____

_____

_____

_____

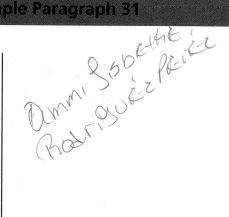

due to: because of

to endanger: put in danger

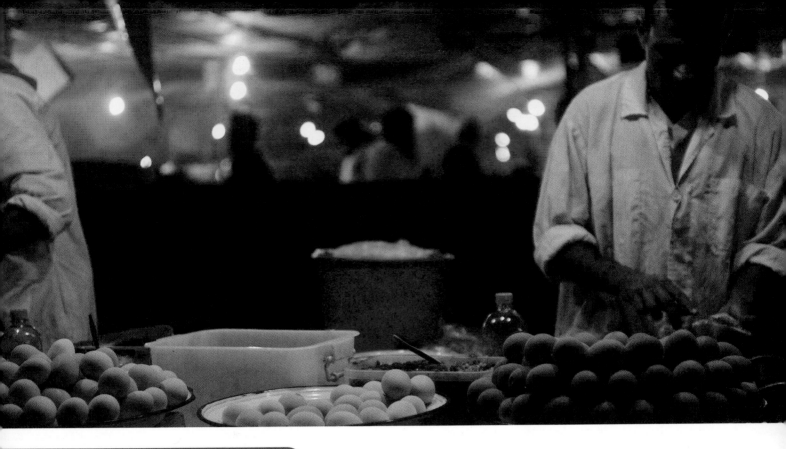

Four Ways to Cook an Egg

There are four easy ways to prepare a delicious egg. Some people believe that brown eggs taste better than white eggs. The first and probably the easiest way is to boil an egg. Just drop the egg into a pot of water and boil it for five minutes. Another easy way is to **scramble** an egg. All you need is a fork to beat the egg **mixture** before you put it into the hot frying pan. A third way is to fry an egg "over easy." This **involves** breaking the egg into the pan without breaking the **yolk**. After a few moments, turn the egg over to cook it on the other side. Finally, **poaching** an egg involves cooking the egg in a small dish that is sitting in boiling water. Break the egg into a small metal cup that is sitting in a pan of very hot, **shallow** water. Poaching an egg takes only four to five minutes.

_____

_____

_____

to scramble: to mix, blend

a mixture: the ingredients after they have been mixed together

to involve: to include or contain as a necessary part of something

a yolk: the yellow part of an egg

to poach: to cook in hot water or other liquid

shallow: not deep

Building Better Sentences: For further practice with the sentences and paragraphs in this part of the unit, go to Practice 8 on page 289 in Appendix 1.

Building Better Vocabulary

ACTIVITY 12 **Word Associations**

Circle the word or phrase that is most closely related to the word or phrase on the left. If necessary, use a dictionary to check the meaning of words you do not know.

	A	**B**
1. to eliminate* something	something appears	(something disappears)
2. hardly ever	not difficult	(not usual)
3. huge	small	(large)
4. to scramble	123456789	(739245816)
5. to get rid of	to add	(to subtract)
6. used to go	(went)	will go
7. to view	to hear	(to see)
8. dust	date	dirt
9. a fare	work	travel
10. property	(you own it)	you borrow it
11. in brief*	a few words	a lot of words
12. likewise*	in the same way	very intelligent
13. a beverage	you drink it	you eat it
14. every other	A1B2C3D4	AA1BB2CC3DD4
15. a spot	(a place)	a time

*Words that are part of the Academic Word List. See pages 275–276 for a complete list.

Using Collocations

Fill in each blank with the word on the left that most naturally completes the phrase on the right. If necessary, use a dictionary to check the meaning of words you do not know.

1. complain / collapse   _____ about something

2. consist / tremendous   _____ of

3. insect / reason   a poisonous _____

4. extremely / widely   the most _____ played sport

5. shallow / spot   our favorite _____

6. athletes / effects   negative _____

7. collapsed / logical   a _____ idea

8. do / make   _____ chores

9. careers / vegetables   crispy _____

10. mixture / shallow   a _____ pond

Original Student Writing

ACTIVITY 14 **Original Writing Practice**

Choose one of the topic sentences that you wrote in Activity 5 on page 77. Write a paragraph about the topic.

- In your supporting sentences, answer the questions that you wrote in Activity 6. Remember to write only about ideas that are introduced in the controlling idea of your topic sentence.

- Use the guidelines on page 86 to write a good concluding sentence for your paragraph.

- Use at least two of the vocabulary words or phrases presented in Activity 12 and Activity 13. Underline these words and phrases in your paragraph.

If you need ideas for words and phrases, see the Useful Vocabulary for Better Writing on pages 277–281.

ACTIVITY 15 **Peer Editing**

Exchange papers from Activity 14 with a partner. Read your partner's paragraph. Then use Peer Editing Sheet 4 on NGL.Cengage.com/GW2 to help you comment on your partner's paragraph. Be sure to offer positive suggestions and comments that will help your partner improve his or her writing. Consider your partner's comments as you revise your own paragraph.

Additional Topics for Writing

Here are some ideas for paragraphs. When you write your paragraph, follow the guidelines in Activity 14.

PHOTO TOPIC: Look at the photo on pages 70–71. Write about a place to visit in your town or city. What is special about the place? What is the history? What should a visitor do or try?

TOPIC 2: Write about a person you admire. What special qualities does this person have? What does this person do?

TOPIC 3: Write about a great career for today's job market. What kind of job is it? What skills would someone need? What are the benefits of doing this kind of job?

TOPIC 4: Give some advice about doing something, such as buying a car or choosing a school. What should someone know? What steps should the person follow?

TOPIC 5: Write about your perfect travel destination. Where would it be? Why is this a good place for you to be? What would you do there?

Timed Writing

How quickly can you write in English? There are many times when you must write quickly, such as on a test. It is important to feel comfortable during those times. Timed-writing practice can make you feel better about writing quickly in English.

1. Take out a piece of paper.

2. Read the writing prompt.

3. Brainstorm ideas for five minutes.

4. Write a short paragraph (six to ten sentences).

5. You have 25 minutes to write your paragraph.

In your opinion, is it a good idea to require all students to wear a school uniform? Give two or three strong reasons to support your opinion. Be sure to include a strong concluding sentence.

Paragraph Review

Hikers ascend Carlisle's steep volcano with a clear view of Chuginadak's Mount Cleveland, Alaska.

To review paragraph skills introduced in Units 1–4
To review the use of articles in writing

*Can you write about
something interesting to do?*

Review

In the past four units, you have learned about the paragraph. Let's take a moment to review what you have learned.

Features of a Paragraph

These are the four main features of a paragraph:

✓ A paragraph has a topic sentence with a controlling idea.

✓ All of the sentences in the paragraph relate to the main idea.

✓ The first line of a paragraph is indented.

✓ The concluding sentence brings the paragraph to a logical ending.

Grammar for Writing Review

You have practiced these elements of grammar and punctuation:

✓ subject-verb agreement

✓ verb tenses

✓ capitalization, comma usage, and end punctuation

✓ sentences, fragments, run-on sentences, and comma splices

✓ pronouns

In this unit, you will continue to practice this information through more activities and original writing.

Working with the Structure of a Paragraph

If you understand how the parts of a paragraph are arranged, you will be able to write better paragraphs. The activities in this section review the structure of a paragraph.

ACTIVITY 1 Writing Topic Sentences

Read each paragraph on pages 97–99 and write a topic sentence for each one. The topic sentence states the topic and the controlling idea. Remember to indent and add appropriate end punctuation.

Applying to a College or University

You need to know that there is a college that can work for every student, whether it is a private college, a state school, a community college, or a public university. The first step in the application process is to **compile** a list of schools you want to apply to. Take the list and **narrow down** your selections to a shorter list of five to ten schools, and find out the dates that the applications are due. The next step is to **figure out** which academic records, such as transcripts and test scores, each of these schools requires. Request your records be sent to each of these institutions. You may also be required to **submit** letters of recommendation along with your application. The third step is to fill out the application for the schools on your list, most of which can be found on the schools' websites. You will also most **likely** have to write an essay for each application. Be sure to express yourself in the essays so the reviewers are able to get a feel for who you are as an individual. The last step in the application process is to visit the schools you think you have the best chance of attending. Take a tour of the campuses to see if you can imagine yourself at each school. If you follow these steps in a timely manner, you should get into a school that is right for you.

to compile: create a list of, collect

to narrow down: reduce

to figure out: calculate, determine

to submit: send

likely: probable

The Amazing Capilano Bridge

The Capilano Bridge in British Columbia, Canada, is one of the world's longest suspension footbridges. The bridge is 450 feet (137 m) long and rises 230 feet (70 m) above the Capilano River. The original wood and rope bridge was built in 1889 to help loggers cross the **steep** canyon.

steep: rising with a very sharp angle

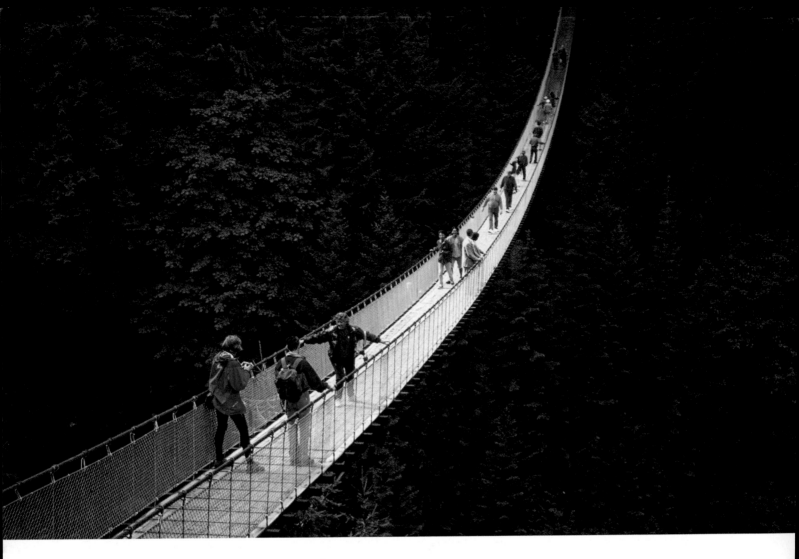

However, today only adventure-**seeking** tourists **attempt** to cross the narrow, swinging bridge. Unlike the loggers, their goal is not to take trees away from the canyon but simply to enjoy Canadian nature. This bridge is an **amazing** sight to see.

to seek: to look for; search for

to attempt: to try to do something

amazing: surprising, wonderful

Example Paragraph 35

My First Time Riding a Horse by Myself

_____

_____

I was excited, but my parents **warned** me about being careful. I woke up early and put on a pair of jeans and my boots, and I **grabbed** my helmet. Then I walked to the stable and greeted the horse. I groomed the horse

to warn: to tell someone about a possible problem

to grab: to take quickly

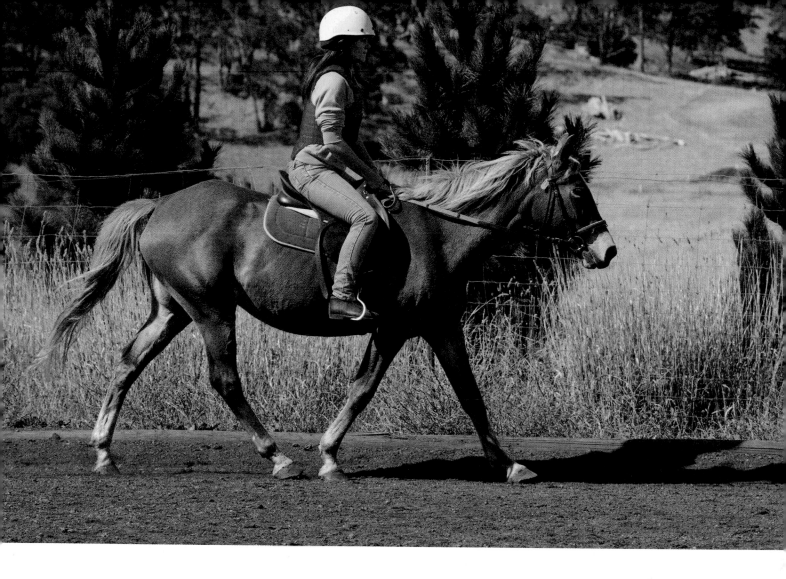

and prepared it to ride. When the horse was finally ready, I walked it outside. It was time for me to get on. I took a deep breath and stood to the left of the horse. Then I placed my left foot into the stirrup and swung over, putting my right foot into the other stirrup. I made sure to keep my heels down and my toes up. I sat up straight and held the **reins** loosely. On my signal, the horse began walking around the farm. The ride was not very smooth. I had ridden horses before, but today was my first day without my instructor, so it was hard not to feel nervous. At the end, I shouted "Whoa!" to stop the horse, and then I got off. This horseback riding experience was fun, and I **managed to** avoid any problems. I had proved for the first time that I could ride a horse all by myself.

the reins: the strings that a rider uses to control a horse's movements

to manage to + VERB: succeed in doing something

Writer's Note

Proofreading Your Work

Always proofread your work – check it for mistakes. Make sure that:

✓ you used correct punctuation and capitalization

✓ you indented the first line of the paragraph

✓ every sentence has a subject and a verb

It is a good idea to have someone else proofread your writing for you, too. Sometimes another reader can see mistakes that you might miss.

ACTIVITY 2 Correcting Errors in a Paragraph

The following paragraph contains ten errors in indentation, capitalization, and punctuation. Read the paragraph and correct the mistakes.

Example Paragraph 36

There is a lot to know about the sport of hockey. Hockey is popular in many countries, including Canada and the United states, the game is played on Ice, and the players wear skates to move around A hockey player can score a point if he hits a special disk called a Puck into the goal. However, this is not as easy as it seems because each goal is guarded by a special player called a Goalie The goalie's job is to keep the puck away from the goal The next time you see a hockey game on television, perhaps you will be able to follow the action better because you have this information.

ACTIVITY 3 Copying an Edited Paragraph

After you have made the corrections in Activity 2, write the paragraph on the following lines. Think of a title and write it on the line above the paragraph.

_____

_____

_____

_____

_____

_____

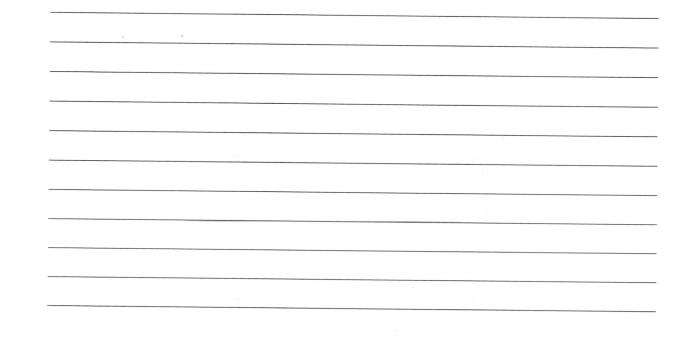

ACTIVITY 4 Correcting Errors in a Paragraph

The following paragraph contains ten errors in indentation, capitalization, and punctuation. Read the paragraph and correct the mistakes.

Example Paragraph 37

Teh tarik is a popular **beverage** that is served in restaurants and markets in southeast asian countries such as malaysia, and singapore. Servers often perform an entertaining show as they carefully prepare it. Teh tarik is made with tea and milk, and its name translates to "pulled tea." To make teh tarik, add four tablespoons of powdered black tea to boiling water Allow the mixture, to **brew** for five minutes. Then pour the tea into a separate cup and add four tablespoons of condensed milk. **Stir** the mixture briefly. With your hands spread far apart, **pour** the mixture into an empty cup in your other hand. Then pour the mixture back into the original cup. Do this several times, taking care not to spill any As you do this, it appears that you are magically stretching or pulling the tea, and this explains the name of this delicious drink. when the mixture is thick and has white **foam** on top, pour it into a clean, clear glass and serve it. Drinking this wonderful tea is as enjoyable as watching someone prepare it.

a beverage: any kind of drink

to brew: cook over a low fire for some time

to stir: to mix the contents of a liquid

to pour: move a liquid from one container to another

the foam: liquid with a lot of tiny air bubbles in it

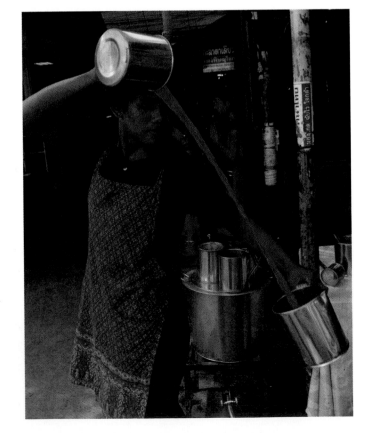

ACTIVITY 5 Copying an Edited Paragraph

After you have made the corrections in Activity 4, write the paragraph here. Think of a title and write it on the line above the paragraph.

_____

_____

_____

_____

_____

_____

_____

_____

_____

_____

_____

_____

_____

_____

_____

_____

_____

ACTIVITY 6 Sequencing Information

These seven sentences make up a paragraph, but they are not in the best order. First, read the sentences and number them from 1 to 5 to indicate the order that they should go in. Then write the kind of sentence that each one is—*topic, supporting,* or *concluding.*

a. _____ During ancient Greek and Roman times, when a new ship was built, a small number of coins were left under the mast of the ship. The shipbuilders did this for a very special reason.

Kind of sentences: _____

b. _____ Today scientists find evidence of this long-standing tradition in a variety of locations, from the decayed remains of old Greek ships to the still active warship, the *USS Constitution.*

Kind of sentence: _____

c. _____ The art of shipbuilding has some odd traditions, and one of the most interesting of all has its roots in Greek and Roman history.

Kind of sentence: _____

d. _____ It was believed that sailors without money to cross this river would not be able to take their place in the afterlife.

Kind of sentence: _____

e. _____ In case of a disaster at sea, the dead crew needed these coins to pay to get to the afterlife. According to legend, the crew members gave these coins to the ferry master Charon to take them across the river Styx to Hades, the land of the dead.

Kind of sentence: _____

ACTIVITY 7 Copying a Paragraph

Create a paragraph by copying the sentences from Activity 6 in their new arrangement. On the top line, write a title for the paragraph.

Example Paragraph 38

_____

_____

_____

_____

_____

_____

_____

_____

_____

_____

_____

_____

_____

_____

_____

_____

_____

_____

_____

_____

_____

Building Better Sentences: For further practice with the sentences and paragraphs in this part of the unit, go to Practice 9 on page 290 in Appendix 1.

Analyzing Paragraphs

It is important to be able to identify the topic, topic sentence, and writer's purpose in a paragraph. It is also important to make sure that all the supporting sentences relate to the topic sentence. Remember to refer to the controlling idea in the topic sentence to see that each supporting sentence relates to it.

ACTIVITY 8 Analyzing a Paragraph

Analyze the content and purpose of the paragraph in Activity 7. Read the paragraph again and answer the following questions.

1. What is the topic? _____

_____

2. What is the topic sentence? _____

_____

3. What is the writer's main purpose for writing this paragraph? _____

_____

4. Do you have any ideas for improving this paragraph? _____

_____

Read each paragraph on pages 106–107. Decide which sentence is NOT a good supporting sentence. Underline that sentence.

Example Paragraph 39

Japan's Incredible Snow Monkeys

Snow monkeys are interesting animals that live in Japan that have **adapted** in **various** ways to the cold winters in Japan. In the winter, they travel less and spend more time in hot **springs** to stay warm. Thousands of tourists come to see all of the monkeys gathered in the springs. Many snow monkeys sleep in trees to avoid being **buried** by the heavy snow that can fall during the night. In addition, their very thick **fur** can protect them from extremely cold temperatures. Snow monkeys also change their diet during the winter. During warmer months, they eat fruits, seeds, young leaves, and other foods. When these foods are not available in winter, snow monkeys dig for roots or eat fish in the hot springs. These **remarkable** changes allow snow monkeys to live farther north than any other monkeys in the world and make this animal one of the most interesting creatures on Earth.

to adapt: change

various: different, numerous

a spring: a small stream of water coming out of the earth

buried (to bury): covered

the fur: an animal's hair

remarkable: amazing, extraordinary

Bears of the Arctic

Polar bears have unique bodies that help them live in the **harsh** weather of the Arctic. They are large animals that weigh up to 1,800 pounds. The body fat from all this weight helps keep them warm. Their heavy white fur not only protects them from icy winds but also helps them **hide** in the large **piles** of snow. It snows a lot in the Arctic. The bears have five long sharp **claws** on each **paw**. They use these to walk safely on the ice and to catch their food. Polar bears are truly amazing **creatures**.

harsh: difficult, severe

to hide: to make invisible or difficult to see

a pile: a small hill (of books, papers, snow, etc.)

claws: fingernails or toenails of animals

a paw: a foot of an animal

a creature: an animal

ACTIVITY 10   Proofreading for Comma Errors

Below is a writing assignment that a student turned in to his teacher. Unfortunately, he did not proofread it, and it has nine comma mistakes. Correct the comma mistakes and rewrite the paragraph on the lines on page 109. (For help with comma errors, see page 60 or pages 258–259 in the *Brief Writer's Handbook with Activities*.)

Example Paragraph 41

A Great Place to Visit in California

When you go to California San Diego is a great **spot** to visit because of the many exciting things to see and do there. First you should visit the Gaslamp Quarter. In this historic area, you can easily find great food fun and culture. Next, you should visit SeaWorld to see the amazing animal shows. After you visit SeaWorld you should see a football or baseball game at Qualcomm Stadium. Finally you **ought to** see the animals at the world-famous San Diego Zoo. If you decide to go to the zoo do not forget to see the giant pandas. If you visit one two or all of these San Diego **sites**, it will certainly be a fun and interesting day!

a spot: a place, a location

ought to: should

a site: a place, a location

_____

_____

_____

_____

_____

_____

_____

_____

_____

_____

_____

ACTIVITY 11 **Guided Peer Editing**

A classmate has asked you to proofread her paragraph. She wrote questions in the margin about four things that she is not sure about. Read her paragraph on page 110, answer her questions, and correct the mistakes on her draft. In addition, there are four other mistakes that she could not find. Find these mistakes, too, and correct them on this first draft.

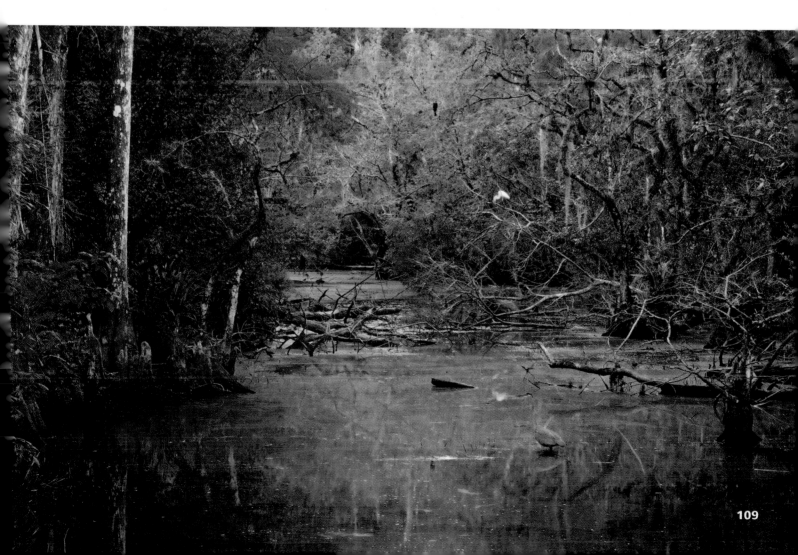

The Florida Everglades

The Everglades region consists of a huge area of very wet land that can be found only in southern Florida. Water is **crucial** to this unique environment This area was formed by hundreds of years of flooding from lake Okeechobee after heavy rains. These floods always provided the land with new water to support its wide variety of plants and animals. Unfortunately people and nature are now taking too much water away from the Everglades. For example the Miami, Little and New rivers all **drain** water away from the Everglades. Even worse, man-made **dams** and canals prevents **annual** flooding, without this flooding or other source of fresh water, the everglades will **eventually** die. Only time will tell whether this unique area will be lost to future **generations** forever.

Should I capitalize "lake"?

Do I need a comma after "Unfortunately"?

Do I need to put commas in this list of river names?

Is the verb "prevents" okay with this subject?

crucial: very important, necessary

to drain: to pass or move out water or other liquid

a dam: a structure that holds back water, usually near a river

annual: happening every year

eventually: happening after a long time

a generation: all of the people born in one time period

Building Better Sentences: For further practice with the sentences and paragraphs in this part of the unit, go to Practice 10 on pages 290–291 in Appendix 1.

Grammar for Writing

Reviewing Articles

The **articles** *a, an,* and *the* are three small words, but they cause many problems for English language learners. Here are a few guidelines to help you as you write.

Explanation	Examples

Use *a* or *an* before a general singular count noun (SCN). You can answer the question *What?*
 	
Use *a* before a consonant sound.
 	
Use *an* before a vowel sound.
	✗ My mother is <u>teacher</u>.
	               _{scn}
	✓ My mother is **a** teacher.
	
	✗ Many people believe *13* is unlucky <u>number</u>.
	                                _{scn}
	✓ Many people believe *13* is **an** unlucky number.

Use *the* when talking about something specific. You can answer the question *Which?*	✗ We're reading fifth unit. ✓ We're reading **the** fifth unit.
Use *the* for the second (or subsequent) time you talk about something.	✗ Dinner consisted of steak, potatoes, and carrots. Steak was great, but I did not like potatoes or carrots. ✓ Dinner consisted of steak, potatoes, and carrots. **The** steak was great, but I did not like **the** potatoes or **the** carrots.
Use *the* when you have a superlative form.	✗ Most interesting movie was *The Hunger Games* ✓ **The** most interesting movie was *The Hunger Games.*
Don't use an article when talking about something abstract.	✓ **Learning** is fun. ✓ People with a lot of **motivation** usually succeed.
Don't use *the* with general noncount nouns (NCN).	✗ All good chefs know that **the** <u>salt</u> and **the** <u>pepper</u> can make food taste better. _{ncn} _{ncn} ✓ All good chefs know that salt and pepper can make food taste better.

When you mean the thing in general, avoid using *the* + noun. It is more common to use a plural count noun (PCN) without *the.*	✗ **The** <u>computers</u> are found in many American homes.
	         _{scn}
	✓ <u>Computers</u> are found in many American homes.
	   _{pcn}

Compare:

    ✓ My mother is **a** teacher. *(general = of any class at any school; answers What?)*

    ✓ My mother is **the** teacher. *(specific = of this particular class; answers Which?)*

    ✓ **A** teacher walked into the room *(general = some unnamed person)*

    ✓ **The** teacher walked into the room. *(specific = our teacher)*

    ✓ Teachers are friendly. *(general = teachers everywhere)*

    ✓ **The** teachers are friendly. *(specific = the teachers at a particular school)*

This paragraph has 14 errors with articles. Add four articles, delete eight articles, and change two articles where necessary. Begin with the title.

Example Paragraph 43

Best Cook in the World

Beyond any doubt, my grandmother Florence Folse is a best cook in world. Many people say that their mother or grandmother can cook a spaghetti, the fried fish, or the beans really well. However, if there were cooking **contest** right now, I am sure that my grandmother would win. My grandmother has cooked for six children, 15 grandchildren, 24 great-grandchildren, and many more **relatives**. She cooks from experience. Since my family lives in the southern Louisiana, my grandmother knows how to cook the seafood, the red beans and rice, and the gumbo, which is a kind of seafood soup. Sometimes she uses cookbook, but most of the time she cooks from memory. If you could eat the plate of her fried chicken or the meatballs, I am sure that you would agree with my conclusion about her cooking ability.

beyond any doubt: with 100 percent certainty

a contest: a competition

a relative: a family member

ACTIVITY 13 **More Practice with Concluding Sentences**

Choose any paragraph you have read in this book so far. Copy the concluding sentence here. Then write a new concluding sentence that works better for that paragraph. After you have completed these two steps, compare your sentence with a partner.

Paragraph Title or Topic: _____ Page Number: _____

Current Concluding Sentence: _____

_____

_____

Your Concluding Sentence: _____

_____

_____

Building Better Vocabulary

ACTIVITY 14 **Word Associations**

Circle the word or phrase that is most closely related to the word or phrase on the left. If necessary, use a dictionary to check the meaning of words you do not know.

		A	B
1.	narrow	not covered	not wide
2.	to bury	in the ground	in the ocean
3.	to adapt*	change	destroy
4.	a dam	across a highway	across a river
5.	vital	you need it	you do not need it
6.	decayed	very new	very old
7.	to rush	fast	slow
8.	a contest	a generation	a winner
9.	fur	on an animal	on a bicycle
10.	a flood	too much money	too much water
11.	to stir	your lawn	your coffee
12.	to hide something	you cannot buy it	you cannot see it

13. to pour	a liquid	a solid
14. to attempt	to do	to try to do

*Words that are part of the Academic Word List. See pages 275–276 for a complete list.

ACTIVITY 15 Using Collocations

Fill in each blank with the word on the left that most naturally completes the phrase on the right. If necessary, use a dictionary to check the meaning of words you do not know.

1. scream / steep   a _____ canyon

2. for / to   ought _____

3. in / on   _____ the corner of 41st and Vine Streets

4. pour / seek   to _____ adventure

5. as / for   a large city such _____ Paris

6. about / odd   an _____ tradition

7. of / to   to find evidence _____ a problem

8. glass / tree   a clean _____

9. about / without   to know _____ something

10. a car / a horse   to get off _____

Original Student Writing

ACTIVITY 16 Original Writing Practice

Write a paragraph of five to ten sentences.

- Choose a general topic and brainstorm a specific idea. You may want to talk to friends or look on the Internet for ideas. Brainstorm what you could write about.

- Make sure that you have a topic sentence with a controlling idea.

- After you write your paragraph, check to see if all the supporting sentences are related to the controlling idea in the topic sentence.

- Your concluding sentence should restate the topic or make a prediction about it.

- Use at least two of the vocabulary words or phrases presented in Activity 14 and Activity 15. Underline these words and phrases in your paragraph.

If you need ideas for words and phrases, see the Useful Vocabulary for Better Writing on pages 277–281.

ACTIVITY 17 Peer Editing

Exchange papers from Activity 16 with a partner. Read your partner's paragraph. Then use Peer Editing Sheet 5 on NGL.Cengage.com/GW2 to help you comment on your partner's paragraph. Be sure to offer positive suggestions and comments that will help your partner improve his or her writing. Consider your partner's comments as you revise your own paragraph.

Additional Topics for Writing

Here are some ideas for paragraphs. Select one of these topics and write an original paragraph. Remember what you have learned in Units 1 through 5. If you need further help, review the writing process in the *Brief Writer's Handbook with Activities*, pages 244–250.

**PHOTO
TOPIC:** Look at the photo on pages 94–95. Can you write about something interesting to do? What is it? What makes it interesting? What can one learn from it?

TOPIC 2: What do you think will be the highest-paying occupation 50 years from now? Give reasons to support your opinion.

TOPIC 3: What is the definition of a perfect parent? What are the characteristics of such a person?

TOPIC 4: Choose a mechanical device, such as a watch, a coffee maker, a smart phone, or an MP3 player. How does it work? Explain the process step by step.

TOPIC 5: The United Nations was formed in 1945 to promote world peace. However, some people think that the United Nations is not useful. Do you think the United Nations is doing a good job? Should the United Nations continue to exist? Why or why not?

Timed Writing

How quickly can you write in English? There are many times when you must write quickly, such as on a test. It is important to feel comfortable during those times. Timed-writing practice can make you feel better about writing quickly in English.

1. Take out a piece of paper.

2. Read the writing prompt.

3. Brainstorm ideas for five minutes.

4. Write a short paragraph (six to ten sentences).

5. You have 25 minutes to write.

What are the best snack foods? Be sure to include a topic sentence, one or two strong supporting reasons for each of your choices, and a solid concluding sentence.

Definition
Paragraphs

World Cup soccer players display joy and
disappointment after the first goal in
Milan, Italy.

OBJECTIVES To learn how to write a definition paragraph
To practice using quotation marks
To study simple adjective clauses
To learn how to combine sentences for added variety

Can you define emotions?

Process Paragraphs

A Compact Muon Solenoid, a particle
physics detector, looks for the Higgs
boson particle.

ME+4/1/03

ME+4/1/02

ME+4/1/01

ME+4/1/18

ME+4/1/17

+4/1/16

Can you write the steps in a process for doing something?

What Is a Process Paragraph?

At times, you are required to describe how to do something or how something works. In a process paragraph, you divide a process into separate steps. You list or explain the steps in chronological order—the order of events as they happen over time. Special time words or phrases allow you to tell the reader the sequence of the steps. The process paragraph ends with a specific result—something that happens at the end of the process.

A process paragraph:

- explains a sequence or process
- presents facts and details in chronological order
- uses time words or phrases
- ends with a specified result

ACTIVITY 1 Studying Example Process Paragraphs

The three paragraphs that follow are about different topics, and each one is an example of a process paragraph. Discuss the Preview Questions with your classmates. Then read the example paragraphs and answer the questions that follow.

Process Paragraph 1

The topic of this paragraph is a popular Mexican dish. People have to be careful when they eat this food because it can be messy.

Preview Questions

1. Do you know any Mexican food dishes? Do you know the ingredients? If so, what are they?

2. Are any of these dishes messy when you eat them? If so, what makes them messy?

3. Name a food that you have eaten that was very messy. How did you eat it?

Example Paragraph 52

Eating a <u>Messy</u> Food

Because eating a delicious, juicy **taco** is not easy, it requires following specific directions. First, you must be sure that you are wearing clothes that you do not mind getting dirty. Eating a taco while you are wearing an expensive shirt or suit is not a smart idea. The next thing that you should do is decide if you want to eat the taco alone or in front of others. Eating a taco in front of someone you do not know well can be **embarrassing**. Finally, it is important to plan your attack! It is a good idea to pick up the taco gently and then carefully keep it in a **horizontal** position. As you raise the taco, slowly turn your head toward it and position your head at a 20-degree **angle**. The last step is to put the corner of the taco in your mouth and take a bite. By following these simple directions, eating a taco can be a less messy experience.

messy: not neat

a taco: a Mexican dish consisting of a tortilla wrapped around a mixture of meat, lettuce, tomato, cheese, and sauce

embarrassing: causing a self-conscious or uncomfortable feeling

horizontal: across, from side to side (opposite *of vertical*)

an angle: where two lines meet

Post-Reading

1. What is the topic sentence of this paragraph?

_____

_____

2. This paragraph discusses three directions for eating tacos. What are they?

   a. _Do not wear expensive clothes because you might spill something on them._

   _____

   b. _____

   _____

   c. _____

   _____

3. Do you think that the writer's tone in this paragraph is serious, angry, or humorous?

   _____ Why? _____

   _____

4. Is there any information that you would like to add?

   _____

   _____

Process Paragraph 2

Preview Questions

1. What is your favorite strategy for increasing your English vocabulary?

2. Do you keep a vocabulary notebook or written record of new English vocabulary? Why do you do this? (OR Why don't you do this?)

Example Paragraph 53

Keeping a Vocabulary Notebook

Keeping a vocabulary notebook for learning new English words is not complicated if you follow a few easy steps. First, you must buy a notebook with at least 100 lined pages. You should select the color and size notebook that you prefer. Second, you have to write down any important words that you find when reading or listening. This step requires you to decide whether a word is important enough for you to

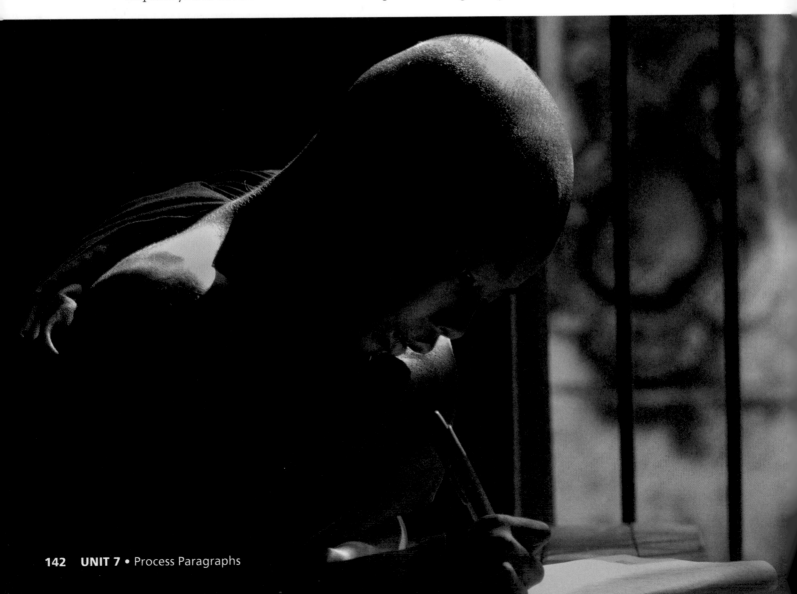

try to learn it by including it in your vocabulary list. Do not assume that you will remember the word later. The next step is a bit difficult because you need to decide what information about each word you will write down in your notebook. Some learners write only a translation of the word. Other people write an example phrase using the word. Some people write a synonym in English. Of course you can write all three pieces of information. When you are trying to decide what to write, you should remember that this notebook is yours, and you should include information that will help you remember the word. You can include information that matches your personality and your needs. Finally, the most important thing you can do to learn the words in your notebook is to practice these words several times. If the pages of your notebook are neat and inviting, you are more likely to review the words and their information multiple times. If you follow these important steps in keeping a good vocabulary notebook, you can improve your English greatly.

1. What is the topic sentence of the paragraph?

   _____

   _____

2. How many steps does the author give? _____

3. Does the paragraph explain the difference between vocabulary you find in reading and the vocabulary you find in speaking? _____ Why or why not?

   _____

4. What are the "three pieces of information" mentioned in the paragraph?

   _____

   _____

   _____

Process Paragraph 3

Preview Questions

1. Describe a magic trick that you saw someone do. Who was it? What did the person do? Do you know the secret of that trick?

2. Can you do a magic trick? If so, describe the trick.

Guessing Your Friend's Number

I am going to explain the steps to do a really interesting math trick that I learned yesterday that will amaze your friends. First, tell your friends that their answer will be three **no matter** what they do. Now tell your friends to think of a number **greater** than zero. Third, they should multiply their number by itself. Next, they should add their answer to their original number. Now they should divide their new total by their original number. In the sixth step, your friends should add 17 and then subtract their original answer from this last total. Finally, they should divide their answer by six. The final result is always three. Your friends will think you have the ability to know what they are thinking, but you know this is a simple math trick where the answer is always three.

no matter: it does not make any difference

greater: larger, bigger

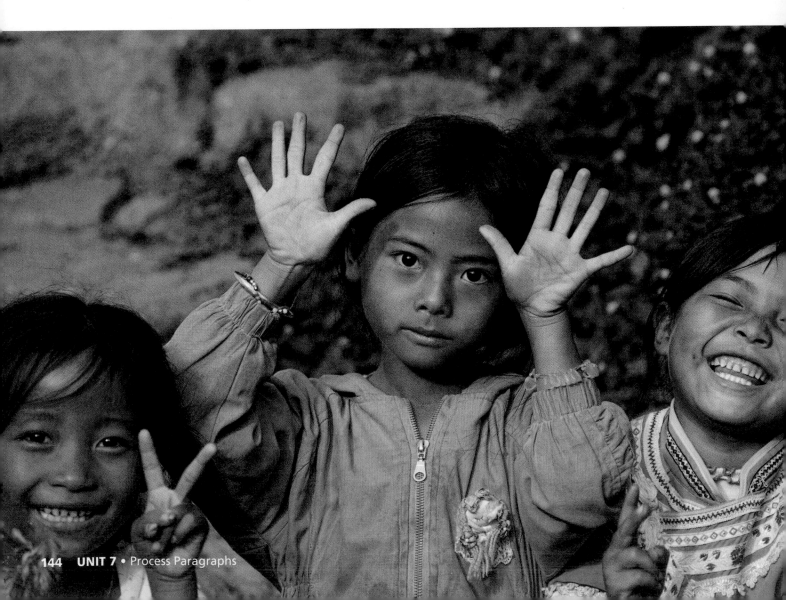

1. List the first three steps in this math trick.

_____

_____

_____

2. This process has many small steps. Good writers do not always write one sentence for each small step. Instead, they combine some steps in longer sentences. Write a sentence from this paragraph that has more than one step in it.

_____

_____

3. For additional practice, choose two steps and combine them in one sentence. Compare your sentence with a classmate.

_____

_____

Building Better Sentences: For further practice with the sentences and paragraphs in this part of the unit, go to Practice 13 on page 293 in Appendix 1.

Grammar for Writing

Using Sequence Words and Chronological Order

The three paragraphs in Activity 1 each describe how to do or make something. The writers use chronological order to show the reader when the steps in the process occur.

To show time order in a process, writers use **time phrases, time clauses,** and **time words** such as *first, second, then, next, the next step, the last thing…, in addition, before,* and *after.* These items are also called **sequence words** or **transition words** because they mark the transition from one step to the next.

Sequence Words	Examples from Activity 1
First, (Second, Third, etc.)	**First,** you must buy a notebook with at least 100 pages.
The next thing / step	**The next thing** that you should do is decide if you want to eat the taco alone or in front of others.
Next,	**Next,** they should add their answer to their original number.
The last step	**The last step** is to put the corner of the taco in your mouth and take a bite.
Finally,	**Finally,** they should divide their answer by six.

Building Better Vocabulary

ACTIVITY 7 **Word Associations**

Circle the word or phrase that is most closely related to the word or phrase on the left. If necessary, use a dictionary to check the meaning of words you do not know.

		A	B
1.	the peak	the lowest point	the highest point
2.	a phrase	right here	We are right here.
3.	preceding*	before	after
4.	a synonym	different	similar
5.	to prove	to show	to try
6.	horizontal	left ⟺ right	up ⇕ down
7.	messy	not neat	not original
8.	quite	silent	very
9.	a jar	made of glass	made of paper
10.	your knee	arm	leg
11.	amaze	believe	surprise
12.	to remind	to release	to remember
13.	your shoulder	body	mind
14.	a stem	an animal	a plant

*Words that are part of the Academic Word List. See pages 275–276 for a complete list.

Using Collocations

Fill in each blank with the word on the left that most naturally completes the phrase on the right. If necessary, use a dictionary to check the meaning of words you do not know.

1. get / put   to _____ ready

2. make / take   _____ a bite

3. down / up   pick _____

4. the Internet / a problem   to point out _____

5. elbow / remind   my left _____

6. from / than   greater _____

7. for / of   he reminded me _____ my father

8. comma / side   the opposite _____

9. tape / tiny   _____ bubbles

10. from / than   greater _____ zero

11. lid / plant   a tight _____

12. direct / empty   an inch of _____ space

Original Student Writing: Process Paragraph

ACTIVITY 9 **Original Writing Practice**

Write a process paragraph. Follow these guidelines:

- Choose a topic about something you know how to do or you know how it is done, or look at the opening photograph for an idea.

- Write some notes about the steps in the process.

- Write a topic sentence with one or more controlling ideas.

- Write supporting sentences that give the steps in chronological order. Use transition words to show that the steps are in the correct order.

- Use at least two of the vocabulary words or phrases presented in Activity 7 and Activity 8. Underline these words and phrases in your paragraph.

- If you need help, study the example process paragraphs in this unit. Be sure to refer to the seven steps in the writing process in the *Brief Writer's Handbook with Activities*, pages 244–250.

If you need ideas for words and phrases, see the Useful Vocabulary for Better Writing on pages 277–281.

ACTIVITY 10 Peer Editing

Exchange papers from Activity 9 with a partner. Read your partner's paragraph. Then use Peer Editing Sheet 7 on NGL.Cengage.com/GW2 to help you comment on your partner's paragraph. Be sure to offer positive suggestions and comments that will help your partner improve his or her writing. Consider your partner's comments as you revise your own paragraph.

Additional Topics for Writing

Here are some ideas for process paragraphs. When you write your paragraph, follow the guidelines in Activity 9.

PHOTO
TOPIC: Write about a process or how something happens, for example a scientific experiment or a weather phenomenon, such as lightning, fog, a tornado, or a hurricane.

TOPIC 2: Write about the steps in writing a good paragraph. How do you start? What information do you include?

TOPIC 3: Write about the steps a successful job applicant should follow. Where do you start? What resources do you use?

TOPIC 4: Write about what you need to do to get a driver's license.

TOPIC 5: Describe how to use the Internet to find the very best price for something.

Timed Writing

How quickly can you write in English? There are many times when you must write quickly, such as on a test. It is important to feel comfortable during those times. Timed-writing practice can make you feel better about writing quickly in English.

1. Take out a piece of paper.

2. Read the writing prompt.

3. Brainstorm ideas for five minutes.

4. Write a short paragraph (six to ten sentences).

5. You have 25 minutes to write.

From time to time, a bank or other business sends a bill or statement that has a mistake. (For example, a credit card bill may have charged you twice for a certain item.) What are the steps in correcting an error on a bill?

Or

What should you do if the server at a restaurant has given you your bill with an error on it? How can you rectify this situation?

Descriptive Paragraphs

The illuminated Jefferson Memorial
is located is Washington, D.C.

OBJECTIVES To learn how to write a descriptive paragraph
To practice describing with the five senses
To learn about adjectives; positive and negative adjectives;
     prepositions of location

*Can you describe an
important monument you
know well?*

Opinion Paragraphs

Giant panda Wei Wei walks around
a birthday cake made of fruits and
bamboo in Wuhan Zoo.

OBJECTIVES To learn how to write an opinion paragraph
To practice writing facts and opinions
To recognize word forms and common suffixes

Can you write your opinion about the best kinds of zoos?

What Is an Opinion Paragraph?

An **opinion** paragraph expresses the writer's thoughts and attitiude toward something. The writer attempts to persuade the reader about a certain point of view. In other words, the writer presents an argument for or against something. This kind of writing is also referred to as persuasive or argumentative writing.

Good writers will include not only opinions but also facts to support their opinions. For example, if a writer says "Smoking should not be allowed anywhere," he or she must give reasons for this opinion. One reason could be a fact, such as, "Over 160,000 people died in the United States last year because of lung cancer as a known result of smoking." This fact clearly and strongly supports the writer's opinion.

A good opinion paragraph:

- is often about a controversial issue

- gives the writer's opinion or opinions about a topic

- explains facts to support the writer's opinions

- presents a strong case that makes the reader think about an issue seriously, perhaps even causing the reader to reconsider his or her own opinion about the issue

- considers both sides of an argument (although it gives much more attention to the writer's side of the issue)

ACTIVITY 1 Studying Example Opinion Paragraphs

Discuss the Preview Questions with your classmates. Then read the paragraphs on pages 182–186 and answer the questions that follow.

Opinion Paragraph 1

This paragraph is about cell phone use while driving, which has been a topic of much interest and debate in many countries for some time.

Preview Questions

1. Do you think that using a cell phone while driving is acceptable? Why or why not?

2. Should there be laws banning the use of cell phones while driving? Why or why not?

Example Paragraph 66

Driving and Cell Phones

Because cell phones and driving are a **deadly** mix, I am in favor of a ban on all cell phone use by drivers. The most **obvious** reason for this ban is to save lives. Each year thousands of drivers are killed or seriously injured because they are talking on cell phones or texting instead of watching the road while they are driving. This first reason should be

deadly: dangerous, able to cause death

obvious: evident, clear

enough to support a ban on cell phones when driving, but I have two other reasons. My second reason is that these drivers cause accidents that kill other people. Sometimes these drivers kill other drivers; sometimes they kill passengers or even pedestrians. These drivers certainly do not have the right to **endanger** others' lives! Finally, even in cases where there are no **injuries** or deaths, **damage** to cars from these accidents costs us millions of dollars as well as countless hours of lost work. To me, banning cell phones while driving is **common sense**. In fact, a **wide range of** countries has already put this ban into effect, including Australia, Brazil, Japan, Russia, and Turkey. Driving a car is a privilege, not a right. We must all be careful drivers, and talking or texting on a cell phone when driving is not safe. For the important reasons I have mentioned here, I support a complete ban on all cell phone use by drivers.

to endanger: to cause to be in a dangerous situation

an injury: harm or hurt done to a body (for example, a foot)

the damage: harm or hurt done to thing (for example, a building)

common sense: so obvious that everyone knows it

a (wide) range of: a (great) number of

Post-Reading

1. What is the topic sentence of the paragraph? _____

_____

2. What is the author's opinion on cell phone usage by drivers? _____

_____

3. List three reasons that the writer favors a ban on cell phones while driving.

a. _____

b. _____

c. _____

4. What is your reaction to this paragraph? Do you agree or disagree with the author's opinion? Why or why not?

_____

_____

_____

Opinion Paragraph 2

This paragraph is about a less serious topic than the topic that Example Paragraph 66 deals with. The subject of this paragraph is the question "Which is better, calling or texting?"

Preview Questions

1. How many phone calls do you make each day?

2. How many text messages do you send each day?

3. Do you prefer to call or text someone when you need to tell that person something? Why?

Example Paragraph 67

The Best Way to Communicate

No matter how much my friends try to convince me that I should text them more often, I prefer calling to texting. Yes, some people might say that using a telephone to make a call is **old-fashioned**, but I do not care. Texting is certainly very common now because it is convenient and fast. However, I really like to call my friends because I want to hear my friends' voices and interact with them. **Without a doubt**, calling is my preferred **mode of** communication.

no matter: it does not matter or make a difference

old-fashioned: old style, not modern

without a doubt: 100 percent, certainly

a mode: a method, manner

Post-Reading

1. What is the topic sentence of this paragraph? _____

_____

2. What phrases from the paragraph show the reader that the writer is giving an opinion and not a fact?

_____

_____

3. Do you agree with the supporting statements that the writer makes about texting and calling? Why or why not?

_____

_____

_____

4. Can you think of at least one other reason the writer could give for preferring calling to texting?

_____

_____

Opinion Paragraph 3

The paragraph on the next page deals with school uniforms, a current controversial issue.

Preview Questions

1. Have you ever worn a school uniform?

2. Do you think requiring students to wear a uniform is a good idea or a bad idea?

An A+ for School Uniforms

School uniforms should be **mandatory** for all students for a number of important reasons. First of all, uniforms make everyone equal. In this way, kids with a lot of nice things can be on the same level as those with fewer things. In addition, getting ready for school every morning can be much faster and easier. Many kids waste time choosing what to wear to school, and they and their parents are often unhappy with their final choice. Most important, some **studies** show that school uniforms make students **perform** better in school. Some people might say that uniforms take away personal freedom, but students still have many other ways to express themselves and their individuality. For all these reasons, I believe the benefits of mandatory school uniforms are so strong that we should require them immediately.

mandatory: obligatory, something that must be done

a study: a research report

to perform: to produce work; to do

Post-Reading

1. What is the author's opinion about school uniforms?

   _____

   _____

2. The author gives three reasons to support the opinion. Write them here.

   _____

   _____

   _____

3. The paragraph states that some people do not think that school uniforms should be required. What is their main reason?

_____

_____

Writer's Note

Advanced Opinion Writing

The most important way to persuade someone to agree with what you are writing is to include strong supporting facts. Your writing will always sound better when you support what you have just written with evidence or good examples.

A second way to persuade someone to agree with the ideas in your writing is to include at least one sentence with an opposing opinion (an opinion that disagrees with your point of view). At first, this might not seem like a good idea, but it is common to state one point of view that disagrees with your own point of view. This is called a **counterargument.** This counterargument is then followed by a statement that refutes, or reduces the counterargument. This is called a **refutation** because you refute the counterargument.

When you acknowledge this other opinion, you should downplay, or minimize, it. One way to do this is to use weak words, such as _some, may,_ and _might,_ as we can see in the following example:

> Some people **might** say that uniforms take away personal freedom, but students still have many other ways to express themselves and their individuality.

In a good opinion paragraph, the writer:

- states an opinion about a topic

- provides supporting sentences with factual information

- briefly mentions one opposing point of view (the counterargument)

- refutes the counterargument in one or two sentences (the refutation)

- finishes the paragraph with a concluding sentence that restates the topic sentence and/or offers a solution. Study this example:

State your opinion →	Without a doubt, all high school students **should** be required to volunteer in their community. **While some**
Give a counterargument →	**may claim that** students should focus solely on their
Refute it →	studies during school hours, **research has actually found** that volunteering improves students' motivation both in
Give your Supporting Fact for your Opinion #1 →	and out of the classroom. **In a recent poll** by the student council, 71 percent of students who volunteered were
Give your Supporting Fact for your Opinion #2 →	better able to manage their time and grades. **Furthermore, students at Western High School have overwhelmingly reported** that they felt like they were part of something greater and could see how their efforts could truly help
State your conclusion →	those around them. **Based on** all of the research and results, schools **should** require students to volunteer.

Facts and Opinions

A **fact** is information that can be verified or proved. A fact is always true. In contrast, an **opinion** is what someone thinks or believes to be true. An opinion may be true or false.

Facts	Opinions
Orlando is located in central Florida.	Orlando is a great city for people of all ages.
Orlando is home to several large theme parks.	There are many fun places to visit in Orlando.
The University of Central Florida is located in Orlando.	The University of Central Florida is an excellent university.
The average annual temperature is 73° F.	I like the weather in Orlando very much.

When you write an opinion paragraph, it is very important to include facts. If you choose helpful supporting facts with examples that the reader can clearly relate to, your opinion paragraph will be stronger and you may even convince readers to agree with you. Readers will remember good, related supporting examples, so you should try to write the most convincing examples.

ACTIVITY 2   Identifying Facts and Opinions

Read the following statements and decide if they are facts or opinions. Write F for fact and O for opinion.

_____O_____ 1. Soccer is a much more interesting game to play and watch than golf.

_____F_____ 2. The Nile River splits into the White Nile and Blue Nile in Sudan.

_____ 3. The most beautiful city in the world is Paris.

_____ 4. Citrus fruits include oranges, lemons, and grapefruit.

_____ 5. Hawaii is the best place for a vacation.

_____ 6. The capital of Thailand is Bangkok.

_____ 7. Security alarms are the most effective way to protect homes from burglaries.

_____ 8. School uniforms should be mandatory for all students.

_____ 9. A glass of milk has more calcium in it than a glass of apple juice.

_____ 10. Apple juice tastes better than milk.

Reread Example Paragraph 66 about cell phone use while driving. It contains some information that is factual and some that is the writer's opinion. Find two examples of facts and two examples of opinions in the paragraph and write them on the lines below.

Fact

1. _____

_____

2. _____

_____

Opinion

1. _____

_____

2. _____

_____

Building Better Sentences: For further practice with the sentences and paragraphs in this part of the unit, go to Practice 17 on page 296 in Appendix 1.

Topic Sentences for Opinion Paragraphs

A good topic sentence for an opinion paragraph must express an opinion that can be supported in some way. Therefore, this type of topic sentence cannot be a fact because a fact is not an opinion. A fact does not need to be proved or discussed. It is a fact. If you cannot think of at least two good reasons to support the idea in the topic sentence, then it is probably not a good topic sentence for an opinion paragraph.

Bad Topic Sentence: Paris is a large city in France.

Problem: This is a fact. Does anyone disagree that Paris is a large city and it is in France?

Bad Topic Sentence: There are several types of camels.

Problem: This is a fact. This topic sentence is going to produce a paragraph explaining the different kinds of camels, but it is not a good topic sentence for an opinion paragraph about camels.

ACTIVITY 4 **Recognizing Good Topic Sentences for Opinion Paragraphs**

Read the following sentences. Which ones are good topic sentences for opinion paragraphs? Put a check (✓) next to those sentences.

_____ 1. A hospital volunteer usually has many duties.

_____ 2. Soccer is a much more interesting game to play and watch than golf.

_____ 3. The largest and best-known city in all of France is Paris.

_____ 4. Eating a vegetarian diet is the best way to stay healthy.

_____ 5. Hawaii is the best place for a vacation.

_____ 6. The U.S. government uses a system of checks and balances.

_____ 7. Although Ontario is the fourth largest of the thirteen provinces in Canada, it has about one-third of Canada's population and is therefore the most populated province in the entire country.

_____ 8. Security alarms are the most effective way to protect homes from burglaries.

ACTIVITY 5 **Sequencing Sentences in a Paragraph**

The following sentences make up a paragraph. Read the sentences and number them from 1 to 6 to indicate the correct order. Then write O or F on the line after each sentence to indicate whether the sentence contains an opinion or a fact.

_____ a. The damage of these rays may not be seen immediately in children, but adults who spent a lot of time in the sun when they were children have a much higher chance of developing skin cancer than adults who did not spend time in the sun. _____

_____ b. Too much time in the sun can cause severe skin damage, especially in young children. _____

_____ c. This disease, which can be deadly if it is not treated quickly, is a direct result of the sun's harmful ultraviolet rays. _____

_____ d. In conclusion, the information in this paragraph is enough evidence to persuade parents not to let their children play outside in the sun without sunscreen. _____

_____ e. Although many people enjoy playing in the sun, parents should make sure that their children put on sunscreen before going outside. _____

_____ f. The most serious example of this is skin cancer. _____

ACTIVITY 6 Copying a Paragraph

Now copy the sentences from Activity 5 in the best order to create a good opinion paragraph. Add a title of your choice.

Example Paragraph 69

_____

_____
_____
_____
_____
_____
_____
_____
_____
_____
_____
_____
_____

Grammar for Writing

Recognizing Word Forms and Common Suffixes

Many English words have different forms for different parts of speech—**noun, verb, adjective,** or **adverb.** Some words have **suffixes** or endings that indicate the part of speech. Notice the suffixes in these parts of speech:

Part of Speech	Purpose	Common Suffixes		Examples
Noun	Names a person or thing	-ion -ment -er -ness -ity -ence	vacation entertainment teacher sadness activity difference	In this photo, you can see the **beauty** of a sunset.
Verb	Shows action or being	-ify -ize -en -ate	classify realize blacken generate	The city will **beautify** several neighborhoods.
Adjective	Describes or modifies a noun	-ful -ent -able -ish -ial -y	beautiful different comfortable English financial windy	That is the most **beautiful** baby I've ever seen.
Adverb	Modifies a verb, adjective, or another adverb	-ly	quickly extensively	Susan sings **beautifully.**

Sometimes a word can function as different parts of speech without any change in ending. For example, the word *paint* can be a noun *(Where is the paint?)* or a verb *(Let's paint the kitchen.)*. The word *hard* can be an adjective *(The candy is hard.)* or an adverb *(She studied hard.)*. Always check your writing for the correct word forms.

ACTIVITY 7 Identifying Word Forms

Each item below contains a group of related words. Identify the word form of the words in each group. Write N (noun), V (verb), ADJ (adjective), or ADV (adverb) on the line. (Some items will not have all four forms.) Use a dictionary if necessary.

1. increasingly   __ADV__
   increase   __N__
   increasing   __ADJ__
   increase   __V__

2. believe   _____
   belief   _____
   believable   _____

3. legality   _____
   legal   _____
   legally   _____
   legalize   _____

4. logically   _____
   logic   _____
   logical   _____

5. finance   _____
   financially   _____
   finance   _____
   financial   _____

6. sweetly   _____
   sweetness   _____
   sweet   _____
   sweeten   _____

7. simplicity   _____
   simply   _____
   simple   _____
   simplify   _____

8. equality   _____
   equal   _____
   equalize   _____
   equally   _____

9. benefit   _____
   beneficial   _____
   beneficially   _____
   benefit   _____

10. freedom   _____
    freely   _____
    free   _____
    free   _____

ACTIVITY 8 Correcting Word Forms

Some of these sentences contain word form errors. Read each sentence. If the sentence is correct, write C on the line. If it contains an error, write X on the line and correct the word form error.

1. _____ Many people did not belief the world was round before Christopher Columbus's voyages.

2. _____ She parked her car illegally and got a $30 ticket.

3. _____ Taking multivitamins can be benefit to your health.

4. _____ Students in this class are allowed to speak freedom.

5. _____ During civil rights demonstrations, protesters fought for equality.

6. _____ Babies often speak using simply words and phrases.

7. _____ My sister is a very sweetly girl.

8. _____ Mathematicians must use their logical to solve difficult problems.

9. _____ Taxpayers do not want the government to increase taxes.

10. _____ The company's financial situation has improved dramatically this year.

Choosing a Topic for an Opinion Paragraph

In Unit 2, you learned about developing ideas for writing paragraphs. This work includes talking about topics and brainstorming. One good source for topics for opinion paragraphs is the newspaper or news websites. Top stories and editorial articles may give you some ideas.

Two methods of brainstorming work well for opinion paragraphs. One method is to brainstorm using the clusters that you did in Unit 2. A second method of brainstorming is to make two **columns** about your topic. On one side, list the negative ideas about the topic; on the other side, list the positive ideas.

Here is an example of how to set up a negative-positive brainstorm design.

TOPIC:	
Negative Points	**Positive Points**

When you write an opinion paragraph later in the unit, try to make a list of all of the positive and negative points of a topic. It will help you decide which points will make the strongest opinion or argument.

> **Building Better Sentences:** For further practice with the sentences and paragraphs in this part of the unit, go to Practice 18 on pages 296–297 in Appendix 1.

Building Better Vocabulary

ACTIVITY 9 Word Associations

Circle the word or phrase that is most closely related to the word or phrase on the left. If necessary, use a dictionary to check the meaning of words you do not know.

	A	B
1. obvious*	serious	evident
2. mandatory	possible	required
3. a report	to study	to do again

4. to set up	to design, plan	to change, alter
5. a point of view	an opinion	permission
6. to split	to combine	to divide
7. to ban	to prohibit	to transport
8. severe	negative	positive
9. without a doubt	it is certain	it is possible
10. an injury	an advantage	a problem
11. to downplay	to maximize	to minimize
12. duties	fun	work
13. entirely	annually	completely
14. a voyage	a trip	a subject
15. to convince*	to persuade	to restate

*Words that are part of the Academic Word List. See pages 275–276 for a complete list.

ACTIVITY 10 **Using Collocations**

Fill in each blank with the word or phrase on the left that most naturally completes the phrase on the right. If necessary, use a dictionary to check the meaning of words you do not know.

1. but also / for example   not only X, _____ Y

2. for / from   to protect your home _____ burglaries

3. all / no   first of _____

4. agree / offer   to _____ a solution

5. in / on   to spend money _____ food

6. may / than   rather _____

7. communication / effort   a method of _____

8. damage / evidence   to cause _____

9. fact / issue   a controversial _____

10. doing / to do   to waste time _____ something

Original Student Writing: Opinion Paragraph

ACTIVITY 11 **Original Writing Practice**

Develop a paragraph about a strong opinion that you have. Include facts to support your opinion. Follow these guidelines:

- Choose a topic such as the value of living abroad, connecting teachers' salaries to students' grades, or why young children need their own cell phones.

- Brainstorm your topic. If you want, use the Internet for ideas.

- Write a topic sentence with a controlling idea.

- Write supporting sentences with facts that support your opinions.

- Check for incorrect word forms.

- Use at least two of the vocabulary words or phrases presented in Activity 9 and Activity 10. Underline these words and phrases in your paragraph.

If you need ideas for words and phrases, see the Useful Vocabulary for Better Writing on pages 277–281.

ACTIVITY 12 **Peer Editing**

Exchange papers from Activity 11 with a partner. Read your partner's paragraph. Then use Peer Editing Sheet 9 on NGL.Cengage.com/GW2 to help you comment on your partner's paragraph. Be sure to offer positive suggestions and comments that will help your partner improve his or her writing. Consider your partner's comments as you revise your own paragraph.

Additional Topics for Writing

Here are some ideas for opinion paragraphs. When you write, follow the guidelines in Activity 11.

PHOTO TOPIC: Look at the photo on pages 180–181. In your opinion, what are the best kinds of zoos?

TOPIC 2: Do you think professional athletes receive too much money? Why or why not?

TOPIC 3: Should students have to take an entrance exam to enter a college or university? Why or why not?

TOPIC 4: Should schools last all year?

TOPIC 5: Who is the person that you admire the most? Give reasons for your choice.

Timed Writing

How quickly can you write in English? There are many times when you must write quickly such as on a test. It is important to feel comfortable during those times. Timed-writing practice can make you feel better about writing quickly in English.

1. Take out a piece of paper.

2. Read the writing prompt.

3. Brainstorm ideas for five minutes.

4. Write a short paragraph (six to ten sentences).

5. You have 25 minutes to write.

In many places, the minimum age necessary to obtain a driver's license is 16 or 17. Many people say this minimum age should be increased to 21. In your opinion, what minimum age should be required to get a driver's license?

Narrative Paragraphs

A photographer lets two trained grizzly bears nuzzle him.

Can you write a story about something that happened in the past?

What Is a Narrative Paragraph?

A **narrative paragraph** tells a story or relates an event. Narratives have a beginning, a middle, and an end. Any time you go to a movie or read a fiction book, you are enjoying a narrative. A narrative paragraph can be fun to write because you often describe an event from your life.

A narrative paragraph:

- tells a story
- gives background information in the opening sentence or sentences
- has a clear beginning, a middle, and an end
- entertains and informs
- uses descriptive words to paint a picture so realistic that the reader can almost feel the experience of witnessing the event live

Beginning, Middle, and End

Every narrative paragraph has a beginning, a middle, and an end. Read this example paragraph from a student whose fear of public speaking causes her great grief in her speech class. Then read the explanation of the parts of the narrative paragraph that follows.

Background of story ⟶
(topic sentence)

Beginning of story ⟶

Middle of story ⟶

End of story ⟶

I never thought I could do it, but I finally conquered my fear of public speaking. At the beginning of the semester, my English teacher assigned us the difficult task of speaking in front of the class for three minutes, and I worried about it for the next two months. I have always been afraid of making a speech in public. I wrote all of my ideas on note cards. I practiced my speech with my notes in front of a mirror, in front of my cat, and in front of my husband. Would I be able to make my speech in front of my class? When the day of my speech came, I was ready. As I reached the podium, I looked at my audience and smiled. Then I looked down at my note cards. At that moment, I realized that I had the wrong information. These were the notes for my biology test, not the information about my speech! I closed my eyes and took a deep breath. Without further hesitation, I began the speech. To my surprise, the words flowed from my mouth. Three minutes later, it was over. Everyone applauded my speech that day, and I left that room feeling like a winner.

The Topic Sentence

The first sentence in the paragraph—the topic sentence—gives background information about the story. The writer introduces the main character—the writer herself—and prepares her readers for the action that will come. The reader can guess from this first sentence that the story will probably be about what the writer did or what happened that made her less afraid of public speaking.

The Beginning of the Story

The topic sentence is the beginning of the paragraph, but it is not usually the beginning of the story. The main action begins after the topic sentence. Not all narratives contain action. They may be about a problem or a conflict. In this paragraph, the writer has a problem—she has to make a speech in front of the class, but she is afraid of public speaking.

The Middle of the Story

After the beginning part, you will find the middle part of the story. The middle part is where the main action or problem occurs. In this paragraph, that action or problem is the speech. When the writer stood in front of the class, she discovered that she had biology notes instead of speech notes.

The End of the Story

The end of the story gives the final action or result. If there is a problem or conflict in the story, the solution is presented here. In this paragraph, the story has a happy ending. Because the writer had practiced the speech so many times, she was able to remember it without her notes. The writer learned that she had the ability to make a speech in front of a group.

Discuss the Preview Questions with your classmates. Then read the example paragraphs on pages 202–206 and answer the questions that follow.

Narrative Paragraph 1

The following paragraph is a personal story about a time when the writer was scared.

Preview Questions

1. Have you ever felt really scared? Describe the situation.

2. What was going on around you during the scary event? Give some adjectives that describe the surroundings.

3. How did the situation end?

Example Paragraph 71

My Department Store Nightmare

I will never forget the first time I got lost in New York City. I was traveling with my parents during winter vacation. We were in an incredibly large department store, and I was so excited to see such a huge place. Suddenly I turned around to ask my mom something, but she was gone! I began crying and screaming **at the top of my lungs**. A salesclerk came up to me and asked if I was OK. She got on the public address system and **notified** the customers that a little boy with blue jeans and a red cap was lost. Two minutes later, my mom and dad came running toward me. We all cried and hugged each other. This story took place over 20 years ago, but every time that I see a department store, I am reminded of that terrified little boy.

at the top of my lungs: very loudly

to notify: to give information

Post-Reading

1. What is the topic sentence of this paragraph? _____

_____

2. Where does the story take place? _____

3. What is the beginning of the story? *(Circle one.)*

   a. He was in a large New York department store.   **b.** A salesclerk spoke to him.

4. What is the middle of the story? *(Circle one.)*

   a. He bought some jeans and a cap.   **b.** He got separated from his parents.

5. What is the end of the story? *(Circle one.)*

   a. His parents found him.   **b.** The size of the store scared him.

6. What is the writer's purpose for writing this paragraph? _____

_____

Narrative Paragraph 2

The paragraph on the next page deals with an embarrassing moment in the writer's life.

Preview Questions

1. Think of an embarrassing moment in your life. What happened? What was the result?

2. Imagine that you are a server in a restaurant. What do you think is the most embarrassing thing that could happen to you in this job?

Talent Show <u>Disaster</u>

My most **embarrassing** moment happened during a talent show at my high school. Many other students chose to play a musical instrument, do a magic trick, or tell a joke, but I decided to sing my favorite song. I had practiced the song for many weeks and could sing it perfectly. However, this day did not go as I had planned. When my name was called, I walked on the **stage** and the curtains opened. All of a sudden, 300 people were watching me. I held the microphone in my hand, but my hands were shaking. Then the music came on. When it was time for me to sing, I forgot the song **lyrics** and missed the entire first part. Then I sang the **chorus** horribly. The **audience** tried not to laugh, but I was so embarrassed! When the song ended, I did not look at the audience and ran off the stage in **tears**.

a disaster: a complete failure

embarrassing: causing someone to feel uncomfortable

the stage: a raised area in a building or a room where people make speeches or perform

the lyrics: the words of a song

the chorus: the part of a song that repeats

the audience: a group of people who watch a show or other public event

a tear: water from your eyes when you cry

1. What is the topic sentence? _____

   _____

2. Why was the writer embarrassed? _____

   _____

   _____

3. What is the beginning of the story? (*Circle one.*)

   a. She was embarrassed.   **b.** She chose to do a song.

4. What is the middle of the story? (*Circle one.*)

   a. She could not remember the words.   **b.** She wanted to change the words.

5. What is the end of the story? (*Circle one.*)

   a. She left the room quickly.   **b.** She helped some of the audience.

6. What is the writer's purpose for writing this story? _____

   _____

   _____

Narrative Paragraph 3

The example narrative on the next page tells about a time in a boy's life when he was unhappy. He learned an important lesson from his unhappiness.

Preview Questions

1. Think of your best friend. How long have you been best friends?

2. What are the most important qualities in a friend?

3. Have you ever moved away and had to make new friends? Describe the situation. Was it easy? If not, how did you overcome this situation?

A Lesson in Friendship

I learned the hard way how to make friends in a new school. At my old school in Toronto, I was on the football and track teams, so I was very popular and had lots of friends. Everything changed when I was 16 years old because my parents decided to move to Florida. Going to a new school was not easy for me. The first few days in my new school were extremely difficult. The class schedule was different, and the teachers were more informal than in my old school. All the students dressed **casually** in shorts and T-shirts instead of a school uniform. Some kids tried to be nice to me, but I did not want to talk to them. To me, they looked and acted **funny**! After a few weeks, I realized that no one even tried to talk to me anymore. I began to feel lonely. Two months passed before I got the courage to talk to a few classmates. Finally, I realized that they were normal people, just like me. I began to develop some **relationships** and eventually some good friendships. I learned a **valuable** lesson about making friends that year.

casually: informally

funny: strange

a relationship: a friendship

valuable: important

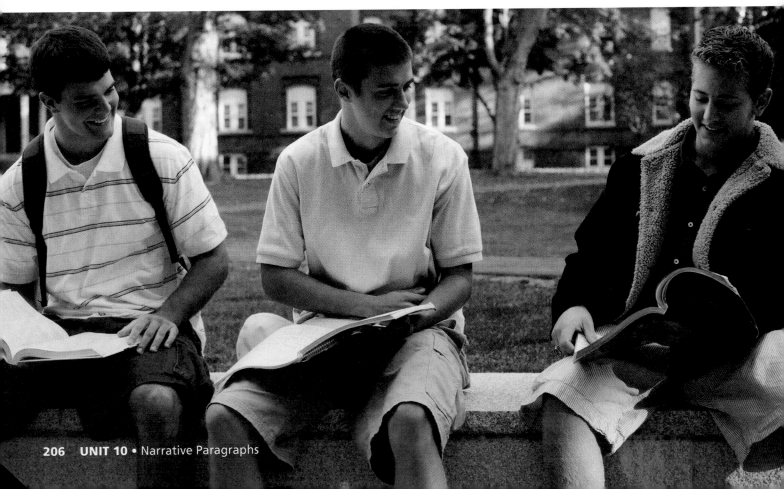

Post-Reading

1. What is the general topic of this paragraph? _____
   _____

2. What is the topic sentence? _____
   _____

3. In your own words, what is the beginning of the story?
   _____
   _____
   _____
   _____

4. In your own words, what is the middle of the story?
   _____
   _____
   _____
   _____

5. In your own words, what is the end of the story?
   _____
   _____
   _____
   _____

6. What lesson did the writer learn from this experience?
   _____
   _____
   _____
   _____

Working with Ideas for Narrative Paragraphs

You can find stories from your own memories and experiences. Many times, the best narrative stories are about real events that actually happened to someone. In fact, there is an expression in English that "truth is stranger than fiction," which means that it is sometimes more difficult to invent a story ("fiction") than to tell about something that actually happened ("truth").

ACTIVITY 2 **Recognizing Good Topics for Narrative Paragraphs**

Read the following paragraph titles. Put a check (✓) next to the titles that you think would make good narrative paragraphs. Be prepared to explain your choices.

_____ My Best Friend, Luke   _____ Natural Disasters

_____ How to Become a Doctor   _____ Bears

_____ The Day I Almost Died   _____ A Wonderful Day in the Mountains

Compare your choices with a classmate. Do you agree on which titles would make the best narrative paragraphs? Explain why or why not.

Using Descriptive Language to Help Readers See Your Story

In narrative writing, you want the readers to be able to imagine that they are actually in the story with you. In order to accomplish this goal, you need to describe your story and your experiences as carefully as possible. Use specific vocabulary to help your readers imagine that they are actually there with you in your story. Your goal is to make your readers understand why this event is so special or significant for you.

Sentence	General Vocabulary	More Descriptive Vocabulary
The movie was _____.	nice	interesting, thrilling, inspiring, heart-warming, superb
These essays are _____.	bad	boring, horrible, empty, dull, shocking, violent
I felt _____.	good	marvelous, fantastic, elated, wonderful, relaxed
We were _____.	afraid	terrified, anxious, alarmed, scared, petrified

ACTIVITY 3 Describing a Moment

Think about a moment in your life where something interesting or unusual happened, or look at the photograph for ideas. What was happening before that moment, during that moment, and right after that moment? Write some details about that moment, including the place, things that happened, your feelings, and how you feel today. Use descriptive language.

Moment: _____

Where were you? _____

What happened?   Before: _____

_____

During: _____

_____

After: _____

_____

What were you feeling?   Before: _____

_____

During: _____

_____

After: _____

_____

Your overall impression or feeling: _____

ACTIVITY 4 **Sequencing Sentences in a Paragraph**

These sentences form a narrative of a personal experience with death. Read the sentences and number them from 1 to 7 to indicate the best order.

_____ **a.** At 7:18 the next morning, a severe earthquake measuring 8.1 on the Richter scale hit Mexico City. I was asleep, but the violent side-to-side movement of my bed woke me up. Then I could hear the rumble of the building as it was shaking.

_____ **b.** As I was trying to stand up, I could hear the walls of the building cracking. I was on the third floor of a six-story building, and I thought the building was going to collapse. I really believed that I was going to die.

_____ **c.** I flew to Mexico City on September 17. The first two days were uneventful.

_____ **d.** My trip to Mexico City in September 1985 was not my first visit there, but this unforgettable trip helped me realize something about life.

_____ **e.** I visited a few friends and did a little sightseeing. On the evening of the eighteenth, I had a late dinner with some friends that I had not seen in several years. After a very peaceful evening, I returned to my hotel and quickly fell asleep.

_____ **f.** In the end, approximately 5,000 people died in this terrible tragedy, but I was lucky enough not to be among them. This unexpected disaster taught me that life can be over at any minute, so it is important for us to live every day as if it is our last.

_____ **g.** When I looked at my room, I could see that the floor was moving up and down like water in the ocean. Because the doorway is often the strongest part of a building, I tried to stand up in the doorway of the bathroom.

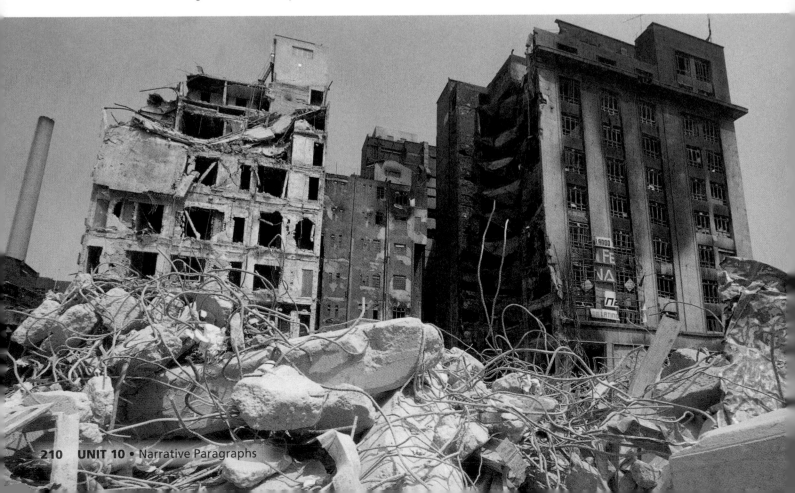

Now copy the sentences from Activity 4 in the best order for a narrative paragraph. Add a title of your choice.

Example Paragraph 74

Title _____

Background
information
(topic sentence) _____

_____

_____

Beginning of story _____

_____

_____

_____

_____

Middle of story _____

_____

_____

_____

_____

_____

_____

_____

End of story _____

_____

_____

_____

_____

For further practice with the sentences and paragraphs in this part of the unit, go to Practice 19 on pages 297–298 in Appendix 1.

Grammar for Writing

Maintaining Verb Tense Consistency

When writers tell a story, they usually use the simple past tense and perhaps the past progressive tense. Be careful to keep the verb tense consistent, or the same. For example, if your story begins with the simple past tense, do not suddenly switch to the simple present tense and then go back to the simple past tense.

Explanation	Examples
Use the **present tense** to show a general truth or activity.	My friends **live** in Mexico.
Use the **present progressive tense** to show an action that is in progress at this moment.	My friends **are living** in Mexico now.
Use the **simple past tense** to show that something happened in the past.	My friends **lived** in Mexico in 1985.
Use the **past progressive tense** to show that something was in progress at a specific time.	My friends **were living** in Mexico when the earthquake happened.

ACTIVITY 6   Identifying Verb Tenses

Read this narrative paragraph. Circle the verbs. The verbs in the first two sentences have been done for you. Then answer the questions that follow.

Example Paragraph 75

Ali's Surprise

Ali (knew) how difficult it (was) to get a student visa for the United States. However, he (gathered) all the important paperwork, including his I–20 document, passport, bank statements, and even a letter from his doctor. On the cold morning of his interview, he jumped on a bus to the capital. For five long hours, he rode in silence, looked out the window at the gray landscape, and wondered about the interview. When he arrived at the embassy, he saw a line of more than 100 people. He patiently waited until a guard gave him a number to enter the warm building. The faces of the embassy personnel frightened him, except for an older woman who reminded him of his grandmother. She was working at window number 4. He hoped that she would be the one to look at his paperwork. When it was his turn, he looked up quickly. A baby-faced worker at window number 3 was calling him to come up. Ali stepped up to the window and gave all his documents to the young embassy employee. He glanced at "Grandma" and thought his chance was gone. Then he heard her message to another man, "You will not get a visa in a thousand years! Next in line, please." Ali was shocked. He turned to the embassy worker in front of him. The worker said, "Here you are, sir. Your student visa is valid for one year." Ali could not believe it. The impossible had happened. Happily, he took his passport and left the building.

1. What tense is used for most of the verbs in this paragraph? _____

2. A few of the verbs are not in this tense. Can you explain this ? _____

_____

_____

_____

Read the following narrative paragraph. Circle all the verbs. Then make corrections so that all the verbs are in a tense that expresses past time—either the simple past tense or the past progressive tense.

Example Paragraph 76

My First Job

The happiest day of my life is when I get my first job last year. After college, I try and try for six months to get a job with an advertising firm, but my luck is bad. Finally, one day while I am eating a sandwich in a downtown coffee shop, my luck will begin to change. A young woman who is sitting next to me asks if she could read my newspaper. I say OK, and we start talking. She begins to tell me that she is an executive in a huge advertising company and is looking for an assistant. I will tell her that I am very interested in mass communications and study it for four years at the university. She gives me her business card, and within one week, I am her administrative assistant. It is the best lunch of my life!

Editing Narrative Paragraphs

Read the teacher's four comments below and the four narrative paragraphs on pages 216–218. Match each teacher comment to the correction needed in each paragraph. Write the number on the line at the end of the paragraph.

Teacher Comments

1. *Your first sentence is too specific to be a topic sentence. Who is "her"? Your topic sentence should tell the reader what the paragraph is going to be about.*

2. *Be careful with verbs. The verbs you used jump from the simple present to the simple past tense.*

3. *Your paragraph is good. However, you didn't indent the first line of your paragraph. Be careful with correct paragraph form.*

4. *This isn't a narrative paragraph—it is a descriptive one. Follow directions more carefully.*

A Problem with My Creation

I took pottery lessons with her for many years, but this one time her advice led to a disaster. I made a **vase** from clay that weighed about five pounds. The clay was very wet when I finished, and it needed to dry before I could put the vase in the oven. I asked her how long I had to wait, and she told me about one week. Because it was my first time making such a large vase, I did **not think twice about** her advice. However, one week later, my vase was still wet. She put it in the oven anyway. Not long after, we heard a loud popping noise. It scared both of us, and we ran to the oven to see what was wrong. When she finally opened the oven, pieces of clay were everywhere. Because there were too many air bubbles in the wet clay, my vase exploded. It was the most terrible incident ever! After we cleaned up the mess, my pottery teacher **apologized** and said she would help me make another vase.

a vase: a container for flowers and water

to not think twice about something: do something without thinking

to apologize: say you are sorry

Teacher Comment: _____

My Favorite Place

My bedroom is small but comfortable. The walls are covered with posters and banners of my favorite sports teams. On the left side, there is a small bed that I have had since I was ten years old. Next to the bed is my dresser. It is blue and white with gold **knobs**. Beside the dresser is my bookshelf, which holds most of my schoolbooks, dictionaries, and novels. Across from the bookshelf, you can see my closet. It is too small to hold all my clothes, so I hang some of my stuff on my chair. The clothes get **wrinkled** there, but I do not mind. My mom does not like it that my room is so messy, so one of these days I am going to clean it up and make her happy.

a knob: a small round handle on a drawer or door

wrinkled: not smooth, with lines

Teacher Comment: _____

A Travel Nightmare

When I decided to travel across Europe with a backpack, I did not think I would meet the local police. My best friend and I were sitting in Frankfurt on a train bound for Paris when the nightmare began. A young man comes to the window of the train and asks me what time the train leaves. It took us only ten seconds to open the window and answer him. When we turned away from the window and sat down in our seats, we noticed that our backpacks were missing. Quickly, we got off the train and went to the police headquarters inside the station. We explained what happened. The police officers did not look surprised. They say it is a common way of stealing bags. One person stays outside the train and asks a passenger for help or information. While the passenger is talking to this person, someone else comes quietly into the train car and steals bags, purses, or other valuables. The team players are so good at it that they can steal what they want in less than three seconds. The police officers tell us that there is really nothing we can do, but they suggest that we look through the garbage cans and hope that the robbers took only our money and threw our passports and bags away. We look and look but we never found our bags. The next morning, we are not in Paris; we are at our embassy in Frankfurt, waiting for new passports.

Teacher Comment: _____

The Trick That Failed

Twin brothers Freddie and Felix often played tricks at school, but one day they went too far. On that day they decided to try to cheat on a French exam. Freddie was very good at learning languages and was always the best student in both Spanish and French. Felix, however, excelled in mathematics. He was not interested in languages at all. When Felix discovered that he had to take a standardized exam in French, he asked his brother for help. The day of Felix's test, they met in the boys' restroom during lunch and switched clothes. Freddie went to his brother's French class and took the test for him. Meanwhile, Felix followed Freddie's schedule. After school, the twins laughed about their trick and headed home. As they entered the house, their mother called them into the kitchen. She was furious! She had received a phone call from the school principal. The French teacher had found out about the trick! "How did he know?" cried Felix. "Easily," replied his mother. "Everyone at the school knows that one obvious difference between you and your brother is that you are right-handed and Freddie is left-handed. While the French teacher was grading the tests, he noticed that the check marks on the test were

made by a left-handed person." Felix and Freddie got into a lot of trouble
that day, but they learned a valuable lesson—and they never cheated
again.

Teacher Comment: _____

Building Better Sentences: For further practice with the sentences and paragraphs in this part of the unit, go to Practice 20 on page 298 in Appendix 1.

Building Better Vocabulary

ACTIVITY 9 **Word Associations**

Circle the word or phrase that is most closely related to the word or phrase on the left. If necessary, use a dictionary to check the meaning of words you do not know.

		A	B
1.	heart-warming	a bad feeling	a good feeling
2.	valuable	important	not important
3.	grief	negative	positive
4.	a rumble	a noise	a smell
5.	to flow	to move	to seem
6.	applauded	negative	positive
7.	came up to me	approached me	persuaded me
8.	to switch	to appreciate	to change
9.	class is over at 9	it begins at 9	it ends at 9
10.	to witness	to see	to think
11.	to collapse*	to cancel	to fall
12.	scary	afraid	necessary
13.	casually	formal	not formal
14.	a tragedy	a bad event	a good event
15.	to hug	to embrace	to prosper

*Words that are part of the Academic Word List. See pages 275–276 for a complete list.

ACTIVITY 10 Using Collocations

Fill in each blank with the word on the left that most naturally completes the phrase on the right. If necessary, use a dictionary to check the meaning of words you do not know.

1. chance / task   a difficult _____

2. at / up   to set _____

3. deep / hard   to take a _____ breath

4. lesson / nightmare   a valuable _____

5. of / on   What's going _____ ?

6. hear / see   _____ the rumble

7. natural / tense   a _____ disaster

8. shirt / truck   a wrinkled _____

9. ears / lungs   screamed at the top of her _____

10. against / without   _____ any hesitation at all

Original Writing Practice: Narrative Paragraph

ACTIVITY 11 Original Writing Practice

Write a narrative paragraph about an experience that you have had. Follow these guidelines:

- Choose a topic such as your first time driving a car, your graduation day, or a special event in your life.
- Brainstorm the events in your story.
- Write a topic sentence with controlling ideas.
- Give enough background information to help your readers understand the setting.
- Write supporting sentences for the middle of your narrative.
- Check for consistency in simple past and past progressive verbs.
- Use descriptive vocabulary words.
- Write the end of the story.
- Use at least two of the vocabulary words or phrases presented in Activity 9 and Activity 10. Underline these words and phrases in your paragraph.

If you need ideas for words and phrases, see the Useful Vocabulary for Better Writing on pages 277–281.

Exchange papers from Activity 11 with a partner. Read your partner's paragraph. Then use Peer Editing Sheet 10 on NGL.Cengage.com/GW2 to help you comment on your partner's paragraph. Be sure to offer positive suggestions and comments that will help your partner improve his or her writing. Consider your partner's comments as you revise your own paragraph.

Additional Topics for Writing

Here are some ideas for narrative paragraphs. When you write your paragraph, follow the guidelines in Activity 11.

PHOTO
TOPIC: Look at the photo on pages 198–199. Write about a surprising, frightening, happy, or funny experience you have had.

TOPIC 2: Create a short story using an animal as the main character. What happens to this animal? You can tell a story from your own country or culture that you think foreigners would not know.

TOPIC 3: Write about how someone you know got in trouble. What happened?

TOPIC 4: Write about an important lesson that you have learned from a real experience.

TOPIC 5: Write about the most memorable movie you have seen. Briefly explain the plot (story) of the film.

Timed Writing

How quickly can you write in English? There are many times when you must write quickly, such as on a test. It is important to feel comfortable during those times. Timed-writing practice can make you feel better about writing quickly in English.

1. Take out a piece of paper.

2. Read the writing prompt.

3. Brainstorm ideas for five minutes.

4. Write a short narrative paragraph (six to ten sentences).

5. You have 25 minutes to write.

Choose a specific event from your childhood that you consider special or significant. Why do you still remember this event? You might decide to write about your first day of school, a particularly difficult class or exam, a time when you were called to the principal's office for something you had done, or one of your early birthday parties. Describe the people and places that are related to the event. Use descriptive language to help your readers imagine that they were actually there with you at the event. Your goal is to make your readers clearly understand why this event is so special or significant to you.

Paragraphs in an Essay: Putting It All Together

Two Mongolian men talking on a cellphone in Xilingol Grassland, Inner Mongolia, China.

OBJECTIVES To understand how paragraphs and essays are related
To understand the basic steps in composing an essay
To write an essay

Can you write an essay about the effect of technology in rural places?

From Paragraphs to Essays

In this book, you have studied many different aspects of writing a good paragraph, including these five features:

✓ **INDENTED LINE**   The first line of a paragraph is indented.

✓ **ONLY ONE TOPIC**   All of the sentences in the paragraph are about one topic.

✓ **TOPIC SENTENCE**   A paragraph has a topic sentence that states the main idea.

✓ **SUPPORTING DETAILS**   The writer gives supporting details about the ideas in the topic sentence.

✓ **CONCLUDING SENTENCE**   The last sentence, or concluding sentence, brings the paragraph to a logical conclusion.

The steps in the process of writing a paragraph are:

- developing ideas (brainstorming)
- narrowing down the topic
- creating the topic sentence and controlling idea(s)
- writing supporting sentences (developing the ideas)
- writing concluding sentences (ending the paragraph)
- editing and revising your writing

Now that you have reviewed some facts about paragraphs, it is time to study how paragraphs work together to form an essay.

ACTIVITY 1 **What Do You Know about Essays?**

Answer these questions. Then work in small groups to compare answers.

1. What do you think an essay is? _____

_____

_____

2. Have you ever written an essay? ❏ yes ❏ no If yes, what was the topic of one of your essays?

_____

How long was that essay? _____

3. What do you think the differences between a paragraph and an essay are? _____

_____

_____

_____

Getting to Know Essays

What Is an Essay?

An **essay** is a collection of paragraphs that presents facts, opinions, and ideas on a topic. An essay can be as short as three or four paragraphs or as long as ten or more typed pages that include many paragraphs.

People write essays for many possible reasons.

- An essay is a common assignment for students in an English composition class. Students write essays on various topics to practice their writing skills.

- Students also write essays for other classes, such as literature, history, or science classes. In these classes, the essays are about topics in the subject matter of the course. A research paper is a longer kind of essay.

- For students who want to enter a college or university, it is often necessary to take a standardized exam such as the American College Test (ACT), Scholastic Aptitude Test (SAT), Graduate Record Exam (GRE), or the Test of English as a Foreign Language (TOEFL). All of these exams have a writing section that requires student to write an essay.

How Are Essays and Paragraphs Similar?

Essays are similar to paragraphs in a number of ways. The following chart shows the main elements that paragraphs and essays have in common.

Comparison of Paragraphs and Essays		
Purpose of Parts	**Paragraph**	**Essay**
Introduction • Gets readers interested. • Gives the main idea.	Topic sentence	Hook Thesis statement
Body • Organizes the main points. • Gives supporting information.	Supporting sentences	Supporting paragraphs Topic sentences
Conclusion • Signals the end of the writing.	Concluding sentence	Concluding paragraph

How Are Essays and Paragraphs Different?

The main difference between an essay and a paragraph is the length and, therefore, the scope of the information. Remember that the length depends on the topic and on the purpose of the writing. For example, imagine that your teacher gives you the general topic of university education. You are asked to write a *paragraph* about something related to university education. A paragraph usually has five to ten sentences, so you must narrow down your subject to include the most important information in these few sentences. Your paragraph topic could be the tuition costs at the university.

On the other hand, your teacher might ask you to write an *essay* about university education. Your essay will need to include several paragraphs about a larger topic, such as a comparison of university and community college education. In this case, your five paragraphs could be 1. a thesis about the trends in higher education costs, 2. university costs, 3. community college costs, 4. the costs vs. economic conditions, and finally, 5. a concluding paragraph. In general, the topic of each paragraph is very specific while the essay topic must cover a wider scope.

ACTIVITY 2 **Topics for Paragraphs and Essay**

Each pair of sentences is about one topic. Decide which sentence is the topic sentence for a paragraph (P) and which is the thesis statement for an essay (E). (Hint: The thesis statements cover more information.)

1. Topic: Japanese customs

   a. _____ If you travel to Japan, you should first find out about Japanese customs, taboos, and people.

   b. _____ The worst mistake that a foreigner can make with Japanese customs is standing up chopsticks in a bowl of rice.

2. Topic: Education in Taiwan and the United States

   a. _____ One difference between the educational systems in Taiwan and the United States is the role of sports programs in the curriculum.

   b. _____ Because I have studied in both countries, I have seen several areas in which education in Taiwan and education in the United States are different.

3. Topic: Household chores

   a. _____ Ironing clothes is my most dreaded household task because it cannot be completed quickly or thoughtlessly.

   b. _____ The three most dreaded household tasks include ironing clothes, washing dishes, and cleaning the bathroom.

4. Topic: School uniforms

   a. _____ Wearing school uniforms is a good choice for public school students for a number of reasons.

   b. _____ Wearing school uniforms would make students' morning routines much simpler.

5. Topic: Sports in society

   a. _____ In my opinion, there is too much emphasis on sports in our society, and this emphasis has many negative effects on all of us.

   b. _____ One serious effect of society's love of sports is that our children learn that winning is the most important part of any sport.

What Does an Essay Look Like?

There are many different kinds of essays just as there are many different kinds of paragraphs. The following example essay is simple, clearly organized, and easy to understand. It was written by a student in an English composition class. This was the assignment:

> Many inventions in the past 100 years have changed people's lives. In your opinion, which invention has been the most important and why? Use specific examples and details in your essay.

As you read the essay, notice the thesis statement that states the main idea of the essay, the topic sentence in each paragraph, and the transition words that help connect ideas.

Example Essay 1

The Most Important Invention in the Last Century

1   When you woke up today, you turned on the lights, ran the hot water in the shower, put on mass-produced clothing, watched television, drove to work in your car, and checked your e-mail on your computer or phone. Every day we are surrounded by thousands of useful things that were invented only a relatively short time ago. *In fact,* we depend on these things for the good quality of life

Transition Phrase → that we have now. All of these inventions have been very important to humans, but the one that has been the most important in improving

Thesis Statement → people's health over the centuries is the discovery of antibiotics.

2   The bubonic plague, which killed millions of Europeans 600

Topic Sentence → years ago, was nothing more than bacteria. It was spread by rats and

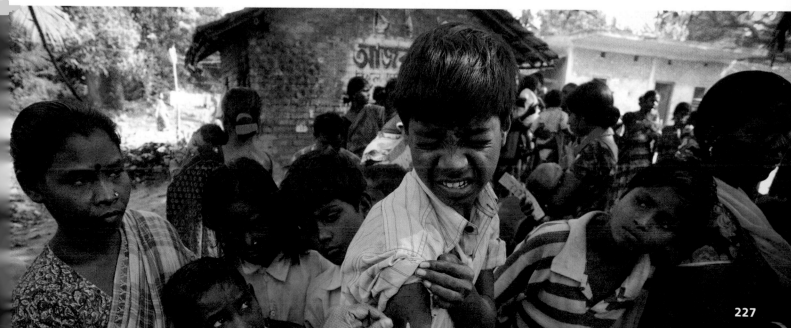

227

fleas. This disease was also called the Black Death because when a person **contracted** the disease, his or her neck and face would swell up and turn black. Back then, no one was aware that this plague could have easily been treated with penicillin. The Black Plague eventually retreated, but people were still in danger of dying from simple bacteria.

3   <u>Even as recently as 100 years ago, medical knowledge was much more limited than it is now.</u> Something as **trivial** as a simple cut could sometimes result in an **amputation** or even death if it became **infected.** Medical professionals knew what was happening; *however,* there was simply no way to stop the infection from spreading or causing more harm. The discovery of penicillin in the early part of the twentieth century changed all of that. Antibiotics finally enabled humans to maintain their good health and continue their lives for many more years.

← *Topic Sentence*

← *Transition Word*

Transition Phrase → 4   <u>*In fact*, antibiotics are an inexpensive and effective treatment for a number of **ailments**.</u> When we have an infection nowadays, we do not think about it too much. We go to the doctor, who will prescribe some kind of medicine. We take this medicine as directed, and *then,* after a few days, we are healthy again. The medicine is probably a form of antibiotics. *In addition,* these antibiotics are painless and fast acting. Without them, countless people would suffer through painful and life-threatening ailments.

← *Topic Sentence*

← *Transition Word*

Transition Phrase →

5   When people think of the most important invention in the past 100 years, most people think about electricity, cars, airplanes, or computers. <u>While all of these are certainly extremely important, the invention of antibiotics promoted good health and longer lives.</u> People tend to take antibiotics and other medicine for granted, but they should not do this. If antibiotics had not been invented in the past century, millions of people would have died much earlier, and human beings would not be able to enjoy the quality of life that we have today.

← *Restated Thesis*

a flea: a small insect that lives on animals; it jumps very quickly

to contract: to get something, such as a disease

trivial: not important

an amputation: the removal of an exterior body part, such as a leg or an arm

to be infected: to have disease-producing bacteria (or similar substances) in the body

an ailment: a sickness, an illness

An Essay Outline

The steps in writing an essay are similar to the steps in writing a good paragraph. After you brainstorm a suitable topic for an essay or paragraph, you think about an introduction, supporting ideas, and a conclusion. For an essay, an important step is to make an **outline.** Here is an outline of "The Most Important Invention in the Last Century" that you just read. Reread the essay before you read the outline. Then compare the essay information with the outline to help you understand its organization better.

   I. Introduction (Paragraph 1)—Many important things have been invented in the last century, but the most important was the discovery of antibiotics.

  II. Body (Paragraph 2)—Hundreds of years ago, millions of Europeans died from bubonic plague.

 III. Body (Paragraph 3)—Medicine was limited until the invention of penicillin in the early twentieth century.

 IV. Body (Paragraph 4)—Antibiotics are currently used for a variety of ailments.

  V. Conclusion (Paragraph 5)—The invention of antibiotics promoted good health and longer lives.

The Hook

The very first thing that good writers do is get their readers' attention with an interesting sentence, which is called a **hook** because it hooks, or catches, the readers. There are several kinds of hooks, and all of them are good tools.

Type of Hook	Examples
A Question	Have you ever wondered how a jet with 300 passengers can lift off from the earth?
A Comparison	My bedroom is like an art museum in any large city.
A Problem	When I won an air ticket to any place that I wanted to visit, I had a hard time selecting my destination city.
A Quotation or Proverb	They say that "the grass always looks greener on the other side of the fence," and there is good reason for people to believe this statement.

The Thesis Statement

We learned that the most important part of any paragraph is the topic sentence. The first paragraph of an essay has a similar sentence that is called a **thesis statement.** It tells the reader what the essay is about. The thesis statement also indicates what the organization of the essay will be. The thesis statement is usually the last sentence in the introduction paragraph. Find and reread the thesis statement in "The Most Important Invention in the Last Century." (Answer: "All of these inventions have been very important to humans, but the one that has been the most important in improving people's health over the centuries is the discovery of antibiotics.")

Now read these examples of thesis statements.

1. Three things make traveling to Southeast Asia an unforgettable experience.
2. Serving in the military offers not only professional advantages but also personal benefits.
3. The person I most respect and admire is my Aunt Josephine.

As you can see, the topics for the essays with these thesis statements range from serious subjects to personal stories. The thesis statement that you write will depend on the assignment that your teacher gives you.

Supporting Ideas

Essays need **supporting ideas** just like paragraphs. Writers should have two or three ideas that support the thesis statement. Each of these ideas will eventually become a separate paragraph. Asking a question about the thesis statement is a good way to come up with material for supporting paragraphs. Remember that it is important to provide specific examples and details within the paragraph.

Here are some questions to ask and ideas to develop about the thesis statements you read on page 229.

1. Three things make traveling to Southeast Asia an unforgettable experience.
   Question: Why is it an unforgettable experience?
   Possible ideas to develop: The people are very friendly; there are beautiful places to see; the food is incredibly delicious.

2. Serving in the military offers not only professional advantages but also personal benefits.
   Question: What are these advantages and benefits?
   Possible ideas to develop: Professional advantages: a full-time job with good benefits, vocational training. Personal benefits: a sense of pride in serving one's country, developing maturity

3. The person I most respect and admire is my Aunt Josephine.
   Question: Why do you admire her so much?
   Possible ideas to develop: She taught me about hard work; she loved me unconditionally; she always gave me excellent advice.

Different Kinds of Essay Organization

Once you write a thesis statement, you can develop your essay in different ways. In the following activity, you will work with some possibilities for essay organization.

ACTIVITY 3 **Working with Essay Organization**

Read the thesis statements of four essays and the outlines of the first two essays. For the last two, write a brief outline that shows how you might organize the essay. Follow the first two examples.

1. Thesis Statement: Prisoner education has succeeded by providing various programs that help inmates be successful when they are released.

   I. Introduction (Paragraph 1)

   II. Body (Paragraph 2): *Program 1*

   III. Body (Paragraph 3): *Program 2*

   IV. Body (Paragraph 4): *Program 3*

   V. Body (Paragraph 5): *One or more examples of a prison that uses all three of these programs*

   VI. Conclusion (Paragraph 6)

2. Thesis Statement: Three things make traveling to Southeast Asia an unforgettable experience.

   I. Introduction (Paragraph 1)

   II. Body (Paragraph 2): *Friendly people*

   III. Body (Paragraph 3): *Beautiful sights*

   IV. Body (Paragraph 4): *Incredibly tasty food*

   V. Conclusion (Paragraph 5)

3. Thesis Statement: Computer literacy is important for children for many reasons.

   _____

   _____

   _____

_____

_____

_____

4. Thesis Statement: The person I most respect and admire is my Aunt Josephine.

_____

_____

_____

_____

_____

_____

ACTIVITY 4 **Comparing Outlines**

Now work in groups to compare your outlines from Activity 3. Discuss how you would develop the ideas in the essays in items 3 and 4 based on your outline.

ACTIVITY 5 **Working with a Sample Essay**

Read and study the essay on pages 232–233.

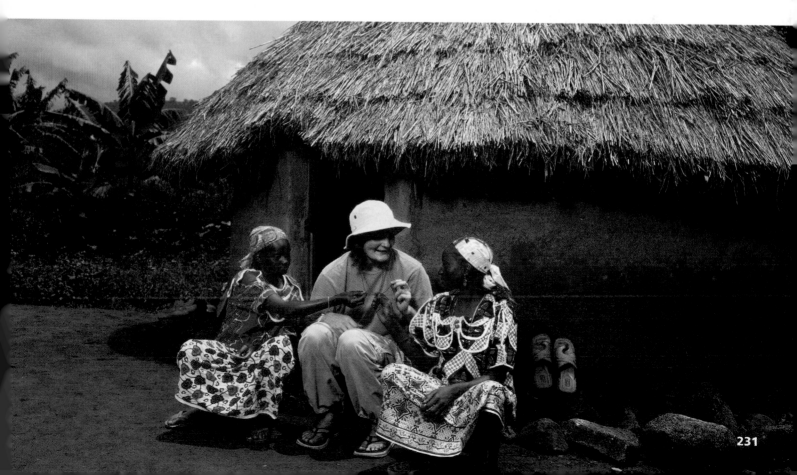

The Benefits of Being Bilingual

1   The Vieira family moved to the United States in 2001. At that time, they made a decision. They decided to stop speaking Portuguese at home and only communicate in English. They were, in fact, living in an English-speaking country. The Vieira children are adults now, and from time to time they travel to Portugal to visit old family and friends. There is a problem, however. Mr. and Mrs. Vieira's children cannot communicate with their relatives. This particular event happens frequently all over the world. When people immigrate to new lands, many of them begin to disregard not only their cultural traditions but also their native language. Over time, they lose the many benefits to being bilingual.

2   One of the most basic advantages of being bilingual is being able to communicate with more people around the world. People do not have to rely on others to automatically know their own language or use an interpreter to get their message across. These bilingual people are independent and self-reliant. In contrast, people who are monolingual must put all their trust in others in order to make communication happen. Bilinguals are masters of their own words and ideas.

3   Speaking a second language also allows people to experience another culture. Even if these people have never visited another country, bilingualism enhances cultural and social awareness of another group of people. Idiomatic expressions, vocabulary, and even jokes can have a powerful impact on a person's understanding of another culture. For example, a person who speaks American English knows the expression "to put your John Hancock*" on something, which means to sign your name. However, only people who know about John Hancock's role in the signing of the Declaration of Independence can fully understand the literal meaning and historical significance of this expression. Thus, becoming bilingual clearly increases knowledge of a new culture.

4   Finally, widespread bilingualism can contribute to global awareness. If everyone in the world spoke a second or third language, people could better communicate and perhaps have a better global understanding of others' ideas, values, and behaviors. Being able to speak another country's language makes people more understanding of the problems and situations in that country. Conversely, not knowing the language of a potential enemy can only increase miscommunication and suspicion.

5   The benefits of bilingualism are clear. In fact, there is no single disadvantage to speaking more than one language. The real tragedy, however, is not that people do not make the effort to study and learn a second language. The problem is that people who already have the gift of speaking another language forget it and lose the ability to communicate in that language because they do not use it.

Cultural Note: This expression has a much larger historical context. When the American colonists wrote the Declaration of Independence, some people were afraid to sign their name because this action put their lives in danger. However, John Hancock was not afraid and wrote his name first on the list and in very big letters so the king would have no trouble seeing it. From this part of American history and culture, we have the modern expression "to put your John Hancock" on a document.

Post-Reading

Circle the best answer.

1. How does the essay begin?

   a. a fact   **b.** an opinion   **c.** a story

2. Reread the concluding paragraph. Which word best describes it?

   a. suggestion   **b.** opinion   **c.** prediction

3. Which paragraph discusses the cultural benefits of speaking a second language?

   a. Paragraph 1   **b.** Paragraph 3   **c.** Paragraph 5

4. Which paragraph discusses the global benefits of bilingualism?

   a. Paragraph 1   **b.** Paragraph 2   **c.** Paragraph 4

5. Which paragraph gives the author's opinion about people who have lost a language?

   a. Paragraph 2   **b.** Paragraph 3   **c.** Paragraph 5

Reread "The Benefits of Being Bilingual" and complete the outline.

I. Introduction (Paragraph 1)

    A. Hook: *Story of Vieira children*

    B. Thesis Statement: _____

        _____

II. Body

    A. Paragraph 2: Topic Sentence: _____

        _____

        1. Supporting Idea: *They can communicate with more people.*

        2. Supporting Idea: *They do not need an interpreter.*

        3. Supporting Idea: *They are in charge of their own ideas.*

        4. Supporting Idea: *Monolingual people cannot speak on their own.*

    B. Paragraph 3: Topic Sentence: *Speaking a second language also allows people to experience another culture.*

        1. Supporting Idea: *Bilinguals have more cultural and social awareness of another group of people.*

        2. Supporting Idea: *Idiomatic expressions, vocabulary, and jokes help people understand a different culture.*

        3. Supporting Idea (example): _____

        _____

    C. Paragraph 4: Topic Sentence: _____

        _____

        1. Supporting Idea: *Countries could become closer.*

        2. Supporting Idea: _____

        _____

        3. Supporting Idea: *Not knowing an enemy's language can increase miscommunication.*

III. Concluding paragraph (Paragraph 5)

    A. Restatement of Thesis: *Bilingualism has only positive effects.*

    B. Opinion: _____

        _____

Putting an Essay Together

Now that you have learned some of the basics of an essay, it is time to practice writing one. In the following activities, you will work with your classmates to produce an essay.

ACTIVITY 7 **Brainstorming**

In this activity, you will brainstorm ideas for an essay that you will write in Activity 8. Read the following essay topic. Then follow the steps below to brainstorm ideas about this topic.

Topic: Living in a big city is better than living in a small town.

1. Form three groups. Each group must brainstorm and come up with as many reasons as possible why living in a large city is better than living in a small town.

   Your group's reasons: _____

   _____

   _____

   _____

2. Write all your ideas on the board. As a class, vote for the three best reasons. (These reasons will become the topic sentences for the essay you will write in Activity 8.) Each group will brainstorm examples for one reason. Decide which reason each group will write about. Write them below.

   Group 1 reason: _____

   _____

   Group 2 reason: _____

   _____

   Group 3 reason: _____

   _____

3. Brainstorm some examples that support your topic sentence (reason).

   _____

   _____

   _____

   _____

4. Share your group's examples with the rest of the class. Fill in the list below.

Group 1 reason: _____

Examples: _____

_____

Group 2 reason: _____

Examples: _____

_____

Group 3 reason: _____

Examples: _____

_____

ACTIVITY 8 **Writing an Essay Draft**

You are now ready to complete an essay. Read the following partial essay and fill in the blanks with the information you gathered. Use additional paper if necessary.

The Advantages of City Life

1   The population of Small Hills is 2,500. Everyone knows everyone else. The mayor of the city is also the owner of the sporting goods store. There is only one school in Small Hills, and all the students know each other, from age six to age eighteen. On weekends, many residents of Small Hills go to the only restaurant in town, and perhaps after dinner, they go to the only movie theater. This routine continues. On the other hand, the population of Los Angeles is approximately 4 million. It is a city that is so culturally diverse that at any given time one can go to any type of restaurant, watch any type of movie, and see countless exhibits and museums. Which type of life is better? It seems obvious that living in a large city full of diversity is much better than living in a small, rural community.

2   First, living in a large city is better because _____

_____

_____

_____

_____

_____

_____

_____

3   In addition, city life can _____

_____

_____

_____

_____

_____

_____

_____

4   Finally, large cities give people the opportunity to _____

_____

_____

_____

_____

_____

_____

5   In conclusion, there are many benefits to living in a large city. While some people might be afraid of existing among such a large group of people, the benefits that a large city can afford its citizens are well worth it. Besides, there is always a quiet, relaxed place, even in busy metropolitan areas.

ACTIVITY 9 **Peer Editing**

Exchange books with a partner and look at Activity 8. Read your partner's essay. Then use Peer Editing Sheet 11 on NGL.Cengage.com/GW2 to help you comment on your partner's essay. Be sure to offer positive suggestions and comments that will help your partner improve his or her writing. Consider your partner's comments as you revise your own essay.

Building Better Vocabulary

ACTIVITY 10 **Word Associations**

Circle the word or phrase that is most closely related to the word or phrase on the left. If necessary, use a dictionary to check the meaning of words you do not know.

	A	B
1. to narrow down	to become general	to become specific
2. aware*	you realize	you do not realize
3. threatening	negative	positive
4. trivial	important	not important
5. widespread*	common	rare
6. dreaded	negative	positive

7. the mayor	one person	most people
8. obvious*	easy to recognize	hard to recognize
9. a routine	usual	unusual
10. disregard	ignore	multiple
11. enhance*	approach	improve
12. enable*	allow	occur
13. potential*	possible	powerful
14. countless	a few	a lot
15. an infection	a health benefit	a health problem

*Words that are part of the Academic Word List. See pages 275–276 for a complete list.

ACTIVITY 11 Using Collocations

Fill in each blank with the word on the left that most naturally completes the phrase on the right. If necessary, use a dictionary to check the meaning of words you do not know.

1. of / on   the scope _____ a report

2. make / take   to _____ something for granted

3. come / know   to _____ up with a good example

4. car / job   a full-time _____

5. of / on   the role _____ education

6. friendly / specific   a _____ example

7. give / show   to _____ a person some advice

8. in / on   an emphasis _____ sports

9. on / to   X has an impact _____ Y

10. danger / tragedy   to put their lives in great _____

Original Student Writing: Essay

Essay Writing Practice

Write an essay about one of the topics in this list.

Narrative Essay:	Tell a story about a time in your life when you learned a valuable lesson.
Comparison Essay:	What are the differences between being an entrepreneur and working for a company?
Cause-Effect Essay:	Why do some people prefer to take classes online rather than in a traditional classroom setting?
Argumentative Essay:	Should high schools include physical education in their curriculum or devote their time to teaching only academic subjects?

- Use at least two of the vocabulary words or phrases presented in Activity 10 and Activity 11. Underline these words and phrases in your essay.

- Be sure to follow the steps of the writing process in the *Brief Writer's Handbook with Activities* (see Understanding the Writing Process: The Seven Steps on pages 244–250). The most important steps for both paragraphs and essays are:

  1. choosing a good topic

  2. brainstorming ideas

  3. outlining / organizing ideas

  4. writing the first draft

  5. getting feedback from a peer

  6. revising

  7. proofreading the final draft

If you need ideas for words and phrases, see the Useful Vocabulary for Better Writing on pages 277–281.

Additional Topics for Writing

Here are some ideas for essays. When you write your essay, follow the guidelines in Activity 12.

PHOTO
TOPIC: Look at the photo on pages 222–223. Write about the effect of technology in rural places.

TOPIC 2: Write about the daily life of a taxi driver. What do you think happens during a typical day? What are some of the joys and challenges?

TOPIC 3: Write about why you think people are getting married at an older age. What are some of the reasons? What are some of the benefits?

TOPIC 4: Write about ways and techniques you use to prepare for a big exam. How do you plan your time? What are your best strategies?

TOPIC 5: Write about the value of competition. What does it provide? How is it beneficial?

Timed Writing

In many classes, you will be asked to write short essays within a limited amount of time. Good writers use their time wisely by reading the writing prompt two or three times, spending a few minutes brainstorming the topic, and outlining their ideas before they begin writing their draft. By doing these steps, they often have time to review their writing before they turn it in. In this assignment, your instructor will give you a time limit for writing a basic essay in class.

Read the essay guidelines and writing prompt below. On a piece of paper, write a basic outline for this writing prompt (include the thesis statement and your three main points). When you have completed your outline (try to use no more than five minutes), write a five-paragraph essay. The total time for all your writing is 40 minutes.

Essay Guidelines

- Remember to give your essay a title.

- Double-space your writing.

- Write as legibly as possible (if you are not using a computer).

- Include a short introduction (with a thesis statement), three body paragraphs, and a conclusion.

What should happen to students who are caught cheating on an exam? Why?

Brief Writer's Handbook with Activities

Understanding the Writing Process: The Seven Steps

This section can be studied at any time during the course. You will want to refer to the seven steps many times as you write your paragraphs.

The Assignment

Imagine that you have been given the following assignment: *Write a definition paragraph about an everyday item.*

What should you do first? What should you do second, third, and so on? There are many ways to write, but most good writers follow certain general steps in the writing process.

Look at this list of steps. Which ones do you usually do? Which ones have you never done?

STEP 1: Choose a topic.

STEP 2: Brainstorm.

STEP 3: Outline.

STEP 4: Write the first draft.

STEP 5: Get feedback from a peer.

STEP 6: Revise the first draft.

STEP 7: Proofread the final draft.

Now you will see how one student went through all the steps to do the assignment. First, read the final paragraph that Susan gave her teacher. Read the teacher's comments as well.

Example Paragraph 44

Gumbo

The dictionary definition of *gumbo* does not make gumbo sound as delicious as it really is. The dictionary defines gumbo as a "thick soup made in south Louisiana." However, anyone who has tasted this delicious dish knows that this definition is too bland to describe gumbo. It is true that gumbo is a thick soup, but it is much more than that. Gumbo, one of the most popular of all Cajun dishes, is made with different kinds of seafood or meat mixed with vegetables, such as green peppers and onions. For example, seafood gumbo contains shrimp and crab. Other kinds of gumbo include chicken, sausage, or turkey. Regardless of the ingredients in gumbo, this regional delicacy is very delicious.

Teacher comments:

100/A+   Excellent paragraph!
I enjoyed reading about gumbo. Your paragraph is very well written. All the sentences relate to one single topic. I really like the fact that you used so many connectors—however, such as.

Now look at the steps that Susan went through to compose the paragraph that you just read.

Steps in the Writing Process
Step 1: Choose a Topic

Susan chose gumbo as her topic. This is what she wrote about her choice.

When I first saw the assignment, I did not know what to write about. I did not think I was going to be able to find a good topic.

First, I tried to think of something that I could define. It could not be something that was really simple like television or a car. Everyone already knows what they are. I thought that I should choose something that most people might not know.

I tried to think of general areas like sports, machines, and inventions. However, I chose food as my general area. Everyone likes food.

Then I had to find one kind of food that not everyone knows. For me, that was not too difficult. My family is from Louisiana, and the food in Louisiana is special. It is not the usual food that most Americans eat. One of the dishes we eat a lot in Louisiana is gumbo, which is a kind of thick soup. I thought gumbo would be a good topic for a definition paragraph because not many people know it, and it is sort of easy for me to write a definition for this food.

Another reason that gumbo is a good choice for a definition paragraph is that I know a lot about this kind of food. I know how to make it, I know what the ingredients are, and I know what it tastes like. It is much easier to write about something that I know than about something that I do not know about.

After I was sure that gumbo was going to be my topic, I went on to the next step, which is brainstorming.

Susan's notes about choosing her topic

Step 2: Brainstorm

The next step for Susan was to brainstorm ideas about her topic.

In this step, you write down every idea that pops into your head about your topic. Some of these ideas will be good, and some will be bad—write them all down. The main purpose of brainstorming is to write down as many ideas as you can think of. If one idea looks especially good, you might circle that idea or put a check mark next to it. If you write down an idea and you know right away that you are not going to use it, you can cross it out.

Look at Susan's brainstorming diagram on the topic of gumbo.

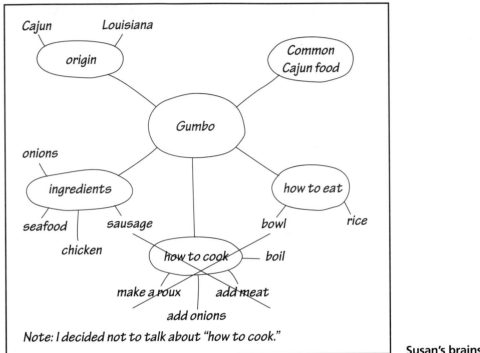

Note: I decided not to talk about "how to cook."

Susan's brainstorming diagram

Step 3: Outline

At this point, some writers want to start writing, but that is not the best plan. After you brainstorm your ideas, the next step is to make an outline. An outline helps you organize how you will present your information. It helps you see which areas of the paragraph are strong and which are weak.

After brainstorming, Susan studied her list of ideas. She then made a simple outline of what her paragraph might look like. Some writers prepare very detailed outlines, but many writers just make a list of the main points and some of the details for each main point.

Read the outline that Susan wrote.

> What is gumbo?
> 1. A simple definition of gumbo.
> 2. A longer definition of gumbo.
> 3. A list of the different ingredients of gumbo.
>   A. seafood or meat
>   B. with vegetables (onions)
>   C. seafood gumbo
> 4. How gumbo is served.

Susan's outline

As you can see, this outline is very basic. There are also some problems. For example, Susan repeats some items in different parts of the outline. In addition, she does not have a concluding sentence. These errors will probably be corrected at the first draft step, the peer editing step, or the final draft step.

Step 4: Write the First Draft

Next, Susan wrote a first draft. In this step, you use the information from your outline and from your brainstorming session to write a first draft. This first draft may contain many errors, such as misspellings, incomplete ideas, and incorrect punctuation. At this point, do not worry about correcting the errors. The main goal is to put your ideas into sentences.

You may feel that you do not know what you think about the topic yet. In this case, it may be difficult for you to write, but it is important to start the process of writing. Sometimes writing helps you think, and as soon as you form a new thought, you can write it down.

Read Susan's first draft, including her notes to herself.

Introduction is weak ??? Use dictionary!

(Rough draft)
Susan Mims

Do you know what gumbo is. It's a seafood soup. However, gumbo is really more than a kind of soup, it's special. ???

Gumbo is one of the most popular of all Cajun dishes.

Combine { It's made with various kinds of seafood or meet. *meat*
This is mixed with vegetables such as onions. *+ green peppers*

Combine { Seafood Gumbo is made with shrimp and crab.
Also chicken, sausage, and turkey, etc. Regardless *ok ???*
of what is in Gumbo, it's usually served in a bowl
over the rice. — *Is this correct? Ask teacher!*

Susan's first draft

What do you notice about this first draft? Here are a few things that a good writer should pay attention to:

- First of all, remember that this paper is not the final draft. Even native speakers who are good writers usually write more than one draft. You will have a chance to revise the paper and make it better.

- Look at the circles, question marks, and writing in the margin. These are notes that Susan made to herself about what to change, add, or reconsider.

- Remember that the paper will go through the peer-editing process later. Another reader will help you make your meaning clear and will look for errors.

In addition to the language errors that writers often make in the first draft, the handwriting is usually not neat. Sometimes it is so messy that only the writer can read it!

Step 5: Get Feedback from a Peer

Peer editing a draft is a critical step toward the final goal of excellent writing. Sometimes it is difficult for writers to see the weaknesses in their own writing, so receiving advice from another writer can be very helpful.

Ask a colleague, friend, or classmate to read your writing and to offer suggestions about how to improve it. Some people do not like criticism, but constructive criticism is always helpful for writers. Remember that even professional writers have editors, so do not be embarrassed to receive help.

Susan exchanged papers with another student, Jim, in her class. On the next page is the peer editing sheet that Jim completed about Susan's paragraph. Read the questions and answers.

Peer Editing Sheet

Writer: __Susan__   Date: __2-14__

Peer Editor: __Jim__

1. What is the general topic of the paper? __gumbo__

2. What is the writer's purpose? (in 15 words or less)

   __to define gumbo__

3. Is the paragraph indented? ☑ yes   ☐ no

4. How many sentences are there? __6__

5. Is the first word of every sentence capitalized? ☑ yes   ☐ no
   If you answered *no,* circle the problem(s) on the paper.

6. Does every sentence end with correct punctuation? ☐ yes   ☑ no
   If you answered *no,* circle the problem(s) on the paper.

7. Are there any other capitalization or punctuation errors? ☑ yes   ☐ no
   If you answered *yes,* circle the problem(s) on the paper.

8. Write the topic sentence here.

   __You have two sentences: Do you know what gumbo is. It is a seafood soup.__

9. Do you think the topic sentence is good for this paragraph? Comments?

   __No, you need one sentence that introduces your topic and purpose better.__

10. Does the paragraph talk about just one topic? ☑ yes   ☐ no

    If you answered *no,* what is the extra topic? _____

    In what sentence is this extra topic introduced? _____

11. Does every sentence have a verb? ❑ yes ☑ no

    If you answered *no*, circle the error(s)on the paper.

12. Write any mistakes that you found. Add appropriate corrections.

    Error 1: _it's-don't use contractions in formal writing_

    Correction: _it is_

    Error 2: _etc.-don't use this_

    Correction: _You should list all the kinds._

    Error 3: _____

    Correction: _____

13. Did you have any trouble understanding this paragraph? ❑ yes ☑ no

    If you answered *yes*, tell where and/or why.

    _____

14. What questions do you have about the content? What other information should be in this paragraph?

    How do you make gumbo? Is it easy to cook? Why do you think people started making gumbo?

15. What is your opinion of the writing of this paragraph?

    It is good, but the concluding sentence gives new information. It does not conclude! Also,

    do not repeat the word "gumbo" so much. Do not use "is" so much! Use other verbs.

16. What is your opinion of the content of this paragraph?

    I like the topic. I think I ate gumbo at a restaurant once.

Step 6: Revise the First Draft

In this step, you will see how Susan used the suggestions and information to revise her paragraph. This step consists of three parts:

1. React to the comments on the peer editing sheet.

2. Reread the paragraph and make changes.

3. Rewrite the paragraph one more time.

Here is what Susan wrote about the changes she decided to make.

> I read my paragraph again several times. Each time I read it, I found things that I wanted to change in some way. Sometimes I corrected an obvious error. Other times I added words to make my writing clear to the reader. Based on Jim's suggestion, I used "this delicious dish" and other expressions instead of repeating "gumbo" so many times.
>
> I used some of Jim's suggestions, but I did not use all of them. I thought that some of his questions were interesting, but the answers were not really part of the purpose of this paragraph, which was to define gumbo.
>
> I was happy that the peer editor was able to understand all my ideas fully. To me, this means that my writing is good enough.

Susan's notes about changes she decided to make

Step 7: Proofread the Final Draft

Most of the hard work should be over by now. In this step, the writer pretends to be a brand-new reader who has never seen the paper before. The writer reads the paper to see if the sentences and ideas flow smoothly.

Read Susan's final paper again on page 244. Notice any changes in vocabulary, grammar, spelling, or punctuation that she made at this stage.

Of course, the very last step is to turn the paper in to your teacher and hope that you get a good grade!

Editing Your Writing

While you must be comfortable writing quickly, you also need to be comfortable with improving your work. Writing an assignment is never a one-step process. For even the most gifted writers, it is often a multiple-step process. When you were completing your assignments in this book, you probably made some changes to your work to make it better. However, you may not have fixed all of the errors. The paper that you turned in to your teacher is called a **first draft,** which is sometimes referred to as a **rough draft.**

A first draft can almost always be improved. One way to improve your writing is to ask a classmate, friend, or teacher to read it and make suggestions. Your reader may discover that one of your paragraphs is missing a topic sentence, that you have made grammar mistakes, or that your essay needs different vocabulary choices. You may not always like or agree with the comments from a reader, but being open to changes will make you a better writer.

This section will help you become more familiar with how to identify and correct errors in your writing.

Step 1

Below is a student's first draft for a timed writing. The writing prompt for this assignment, was "Many schools now offer classes online. Which do you prefer and why?" As you read the first draft, look for areas that need improvement and write your comments. For example, does every sentence have a subject and a verb? Does the writer always use the correct verb tense and punctuation? Does the paragraph have a topic sentence with controlling ideas? Is the vocabulary suitable for the intended audience? What do you think of the content?

The Online Courses

Online courses are very popular at my university. I prefered traditional face-to-face classes. At my university, students have a choice between courses that are taught online in a virtual classroom and the regular kind of classroom. I know that many students prefer online classes, but I cannot adjust to that style of educate. For me, is important to have a professor who explains the material to everyone "live" and then answer any questions that we have. Sometimes students might think they understand the material until the professor questions, and then we realize that we did not understand everything. At that moment, the professor then offers other explanation to help bridge the gap. I do not see this kind of spontaneous learning and teaching can take place online. I have never taken an online course until now. Some of my friends like online courses because they can take the class at his own convenience instead of have to assist class at a set time. However, these supposed conveniences are not outweigh the educational advantages that traditional face-to-face classes offer.

Step 2

Read the teacher comments on the first draft of "The Online Courses." Are these the same things that you noticed?

Your title is OK. Any other ideas?

The Online Courses

Combine first two sentences.

Online courses are very popular at my university. I prefered traditional face-to-face

classes. At my university, students have a choice between courses that are taught online in a virtual

Give more details about CLASSROOM. Describe it.

classroom and the regular kind of classroom. I know that many students prefer online classes,

WORD FORM SUBJ?

but I cannot adjust to that style of educate. For me, is important to have a professor who explains

the material to everyone "live" and then answer any questions that we have. Sometimes students

POSES A QUESTION

might think they understand the material until the professor questions, and then we realize that

we did not understand everything. At that moment, the professor then offers other explanation

Which gap???　　　*HOW?*

to help bridge the gap. I do not see this kind of spontaneous learning and teaching can take place

Purpose of this sentence? Connected to the topic?

online. I have never taken an online course until now. Some of my friends like online courses

because they can take the class at his own convenience instead of have to assist class at a set

Add more reasons here!

time. However, these supposed conveniences are not outweigh the educational advantages that

traditional face-to-face classes offer.

You have some very good ideas in this paragraph. Your topic sentence and concluding sentence are good. Your title is OK, but can you spice it up? It's rather plain right now. Check to make sure that all of your sentences are relevant. Also, I've circled several grammar errors. You need to change these. I also recommend adding some info in a few places. All in all, it's a good paragraph. I understand why you don't like online courses. The more specific reasons you can provide, the better you can convince your readers.

Step 3

Now read the writer's second draft of the paragraph. How is it the same as the first draft? How is it different? Did the writer fix all the sentence mistakes?

Online Courses

Online courses are very popular at my university but I prefer traditional face-to-face classes. At my university students have a choice between courses that are taught online in a virtual classroom and the regular kind of classroom with a room, a professor, and students in chairs. I know that many students prefer online classes, but I cannot adjust to that style of education. For me, it is important to have a professor who explains the material to everyone "live" and then answers any questions that we might have. Sometimes students might think they understand the material until the professor poses a question, and then we realize that we did not understand everything. At that moment, the professor then offers another explanation to help bridge the gap between our knowledge and the truth. I do not see how this kind of spontaneous leaerning and teaching can take place online. Some of my friends like online courses because they can take the class at their own convenience instead of having to attend class at a set time. They also like to save transportation money and time. However, these supposed conveniences do not outweigh the many educational advantages that traditional face-to-face classes offer.

Capitalization Activities
Basic Capitalization Rules

1. Always capitalize the first word of a sentence.

> **T**oday is not Sunday.
>
> **I**t is not Saturday either.
>
> **D**o you know today's date?

2. Always capitalize the word *I* no matter where it is in a sentence.

> John brought the dessert, and **I** brought some drinks.
>
> **I** want some tea.
>
> The winners of the contest were Ned and **I**.

3. Capitalize proper nouns—the names of specific people, places, or things. Capitalize a person's title, including Mr., Mrs., Ms., and Dr. Compare these example pairs.

Proper nouns: When our teacher **M**r. **H**ill visited his home state of **A**rizona, he took a short trip to see the **G**rand **C**anyon.

Common nouns: When our teacher visited his home state, he saw many mountains and canyons.

Proper nouns: **T**he **S**tatue of **L**iberty is located on **L**iberty **I**sland in **N**ew **Y**ork.

Common nouns: There is a famous statue on that island, isn't there?

4. Capitalize names of countries and other geographic areas. Capitalize the names of people from those areas. Capitalize the names of languages.

> People from **B**razil are called **B**razilians. They speak **P**ortuguese.
>
> People from **G**ermany are called **G**ermans. They speak **G**erman.

5. Capitalize titles of works, such as books, movies, and pieces of art. If you look at the example paragraphs in this book, you will notice that each of them begins with a title. In a title, pay attention to which words begin with a capital letter and which words do not.

> *Gumbo* *A Lesson in Friendship* *An Immigrant in the Family*
>
> *The King and I* *The Tale of Pinocchio* *Love at First Sight*

The rules for capitalizing titles are easy.

- Always capitalize the first letter of a title.
- If the title has more than one word, capitalize all the words that have meaning (content words).
- Do not capitalize small (function) words, such as *a, an, and, the, in, with, on, for, to, above,* and *or.*

Capitalization Activities

ACTIVITY 1

Circle the words that have capitalization errors. Make the corrections above the errors.

1. the last day to sign up for the trip to sao paolo is this Thursday.

2. does jill live in west bay apartments, too?

3. the flight to Vancouver left late Saturday night and arrived early Sunday morning.

4. My sister has two daughters. Their names are rachel and rosalyn.

5. one of the most important sporting events is the world cup.

ACTIVITY 2

Complete these statements. Be sure to use correct capitalization.

1. *U.S.A.* stands for the United _____ of _____ .

2. The seventh month of the year is _____ .

3. _____ is the capital of Brazil.

4. One of the most popular brands of jeans is _____ .

5. The first person to walk on the moon was named _____ .

6. Parts of Europe were destroyed in _____ (1914–18).

7. My favorite restaurant is _____ .

8. Beijing is the largest city in _____ .

9. The winter months are _____ , _____ , and _____ .

10. The last movie that I saw was _____ .

ACTIVITY 3

Read the following titles. Rewrite them with correct capitalization.

1. my favorite food _____

2. living in montreal _____

3. the best restaurant in town _____

4. my best friend's new car _____

5. a new trend in Hollywood _____

6. why i left my country _____

7. my side of the mountain _____

8. no more room for a friend _____

Read the following paragraph. Circle the capitalization errors and make corrections above the errors.

A visit to Cuba

according to an article in last week's issue of *time*, the prime minister of canada will visit cuba soon in order to establish better economic ties between the two countries. because the united states does not have a history of good relations with cuba, canada's recent decision may result in problems between washington and ottawa. In an interview, the canadian prime minister indicated that his country was ready to reestablish some sort of cooperation with cuba and that canada would do so as quickly as possible. there is no doubt that this new development will be discussed at the opening session of congress next tuesday.

ACTIVITY 5

Read the following paragraph. Circle the capitalization errors and make corrections above the errors.

crossing the atlantic from atlanta

it used to be difficult to travel directly from atlanta to europe, but this is certainly not the case nowadays. union airways offers several daily flights to london. jetwings express offers flights every day to frankfurt and twice a week to berlin. other european air carriers that offer direct flights from atlanta to europe are valuair and luxliner. However, the airline with the largest number of direct flights to any european city is not a european airline. smead airlines, which is a new and rising airline in the united states, offers 17 flights a day to 12 european cities, including paris, london, frankfurt, zurich, rome, and athens.

Read the following paragraph. Circle the capitalization errors and make corrections above the errors.

Example Paragraph 83

my beginnings in foreign languages

I have always loved foreign languages. When I was in tenth grade, I took my first foreign language class. It was french I. My teacher was named mrs. montluzin. She was a wonderful teacher who inspired me to develop my interest in foreign languages. Before I finished high school, I took a second year of french and one year of spanish. I wish my high school had offered latin or greek, but the small size of the school body prevented this. Over the years since I graduated from high school, I have lived and worked abroad. I studied arabic when I lived in saudi arabia, japanese in japan, and malay in malaysia. Two years ago, I took a german class in the united states. Because of recent travels to uzbekistan and kyrgyzstan, which are two republics from the former soviet union, I have a strong desire to study russian. I hope that my love of learning foreign languages will continue.

Punctuation Activities
End Punctuation

The three most common punctuation marks found at the end of English sentences are the **period**, the **question mark**, and the **exclamation point**. It is important to know how to use all three of them correctly. Of these three, however, the period is by far the most commonly used punctuation mark.

1. **period** (.) A period is used at the end of a declarative sentence.

    This sentence is a declarative sentence.

    This sentence is not a question.

    All three of these sentences end with a period.

2. **question mark** (?) A question mark is used at the end of a question.

    Is this idea difficult?

    Is it hard to remember the name of this mark?

    How many questions are in this group?

3. **exclamation point** (!) An exclamation point is used at the end of an exclamation. It is less common than the other two marks.

> I cannot believe you think this topic is difficult!

> This is the best writing book in the world!

> Now I understand all of these examples!

ACTIVITY 1

Add the correct end punctuation.

1. Congratulations

2. Do most people think that the governor was unaware of the theft

3. Do not open your test booklet until you are told to do so

4. Will the president attend the meeting

5. Jason put the dishes in the dishwasher and then watched TV

ACTIVITY 2

Look at an article in any English newspaper or magazine. Circle every end punctuation mark. Then answer these questions.

1. How many final periods are there? _____ (or _____ %)

2. How many final question marks are there? _____ (or _____ %)

3. How many final exclamation points are there? _____ (or _____ %)

4. What is the total number of sentences? _____

Use this last number to calculate the percentages for each of the categories. Does the period occur most often?

Commas

The comma has several different functions in English. Here are some of the most common ones.

1. A comma separates a list of three or more things. There should be a comma between the items in a list.

> He speaks French and English. (No comma is needed because there are only two items.)

> She speaks French, English, and Chinese.

2. A comma separates two sentences when there is a combining word (coordinating conjunction) such as *and, but, or, so, for, nor,* and *yet.* The easy way to remember these conjunctions is *FANBOYS (for, and, nor, but, or, yet, so).*

> Six people took the course, but only five of them passed the test.

> Sammy bought the cake, and Paul paid for the ice cream.

> Students can register for classes in person, or they may submit their applications by mail.

3. A comma is used to separate an introductory word or phrase from the rest of the sentence.

> In conclusion, doctors are advising people to take more vitamins.

> First, you will need a pencil.

> Because of the heavy rains, many of the roads were flooded.

> Finally, add the nuts to the batter.

4. A comma is used to separate an appositive from the rest of the sentence. An appositive is a word or group of words that renames a noun before it. An appositive provides additional information about the noun.

subject (noun)   appositive   verb

Washington, the first president of the United States, was a clever military leader.

In this sentence, the phrase *the first president of the United States* is an appositive. This phrase renames or explains the noun *Washington*.

5. A comma is sometimes used with adjective clauses. An adjective clause usually begins with a relative pronoun *(who, that, which, whom, whose, whoever,* or *whomever)*. We use a comma when the information in the clause is unnecessary or extra. (This is also called a nonrestrictive clause.)

The book that is on the teacher's desk is the main book for this class.

(Here, when you say "the book," the reader does not know which book you are talking about, so the information in the adjective clause is necessary. In this case, do not set off the adjective clause with a comma.)

The History of Korea, which is on the teacher's desk, is the main book for this class.

(The name of the book is given, so the information in the adjective clause is not necessary to help the reader identify the book. In this case, you must use commas to show that the information in the adjective clause is extra, or nonrestrictive.)

ACTIVITY 3

Add commas as needed in these sentences. Some sentences may be correct, and others may need more than one comma.

1. For the past fifteen years Mary Parker has been both the director and producer of all the plays at this theater.

2. Despite all the problems we had on our vacation we managed to have a good time.

3. I believe the best countries to visit in Africa are Senegal Tunisia and Ghana.

4. She believes the best countries to visit in Africa are Senegal and Tunisia.

5. The third step in this process is to grate the carrots and the potatoes.

6. Third grate the carrots and the potatoes.

7. Blue green and red are strong colors. For this reason they are not appropriate for a living room wall.

8. Without anyone to teach foreign language classes next year the school will be unable to offer French Spanish or German.

9. The NEQ 7000 the very latest computer from Electron Technologies is not selling very well.

10. Because of injuries neither Carl nor Jamil two of the best players on the football team will be able to play in tomorrow's game.

11. The job interview is for a position at Mills Trust Company which is the largest company in this area.

12. The job interview is for a position at a large company that has more than 1,000 employees in this area.

13. Kevin's birthday is January 18 which is the same day that Laura and Greg have their birthdays.

14. Martina Navratilova whom most tennis fans refer to only as Martina dominated women's tennis for years.

15. My brother who lives in San Salvador has two children. (I have several brothers.)

16. My brother who lives in San Salvador has two children. (I have only one brother.)

17. This flight is leaving for La Paz which is the first of three stops that the plane will make.

18. No one knows the name of the person who will take over the committee in January so there have been many rumors about this.

19. Greenfield Central Bank the most recent bank to open a branch here in our area has tried to establish a branch here for years.

20. On the right side of the living room an antique radio sits on top of a glass table that also has a flowerpot a photo of a baby and a magazine.

Apostrophes

Apostrophes have two basic uses in English. They indicate either a contraction or possession.

Contractions: Use an apostrophe in a contraction in place of the letter or letters that have been deleted.

> He's (he is *or* he has), they're (they are), I've (I have), we'd (we would *or* we had)

Possession: Use an apostrophe to indicate possession. Add an apostrophe and the letter *s* after the word. If a plural word already ends in *s*, then just add an apostrophe.

> Gandhi's role in the history of India
> Yesterday's paper
> the boy's books (One boy has some books.)
> the boys' books (Several boys have one or more books.)

ACTIVITY 4

Correct the apostrophe errors in these sentences.

1. I am going to Victors birthday party on Saturday.

2. My three cousins house is right next to Mr. Wilsons house.

3. Hardly anyone remembers Stalins drastic actions in the early part of the last century.

4. It goes without saying that wed be better off without so much poverty in this world.

5. The reasons that were given for the childrens bad behavior were unbelievable.

Quotation Marks

Below are three of the most common uses for quotation marks.

1. To mark the exact words that were spoken by someone:

    The king said, "I refuse to give up my throne." (The period is inside the quotation marks.)*

    "None of the solutions is correct," said the professor. (The comma is inside the quotation marks.)*

    The king said that he refuses to give up his throne. (No quotation marks are needed because the sentence does not include the king's exact words. This style is called indirect speech.)

    * Note that the comma separates the verb that tells the form of communications (*said, announced, wrote*) and the quotation.

2. To mark language that a writer has borrowed from another source:

    The dictionary defines gossip as an "informal conversation, often about other people's private affairs," but I would add that it is usually malicious.

    This research concludes that there was "no real reason to expect this computer software program to produce good results with high school students."

    According to an article in *The San Jose Times,* about half of the money was stolen. (No quotes are necessary here because it is a summary of information rather than exact words from the article.)

    NOTE: See pages 273–274 for more information on citing sources.

3. To indicate when a word or phrase is being used in a special way:

    The king believed himself to be the leader of a democracy, so he allowed the prisoner to choose his method of dying. According to the king, allowing this kind of "democracy" showed that he was indeed a good ruler.

ACTIVITY 5

Add quotation marks where necessary. Remember the rules for placing commas, periods, and question marks inside or outside the quotation marks.

1. As I was leaving the room, I heard the teacher say, Be sure to study Chapter 7.

2. It is impossible to say that using dictionaries is useless. However, according to research published in the latest issue of the *General Language Journal,* dictionary use is down. I found the article's statement that 18.3 percent of students do not own a dictionary and 37.2 percent never use their dictionary (p. 75) to be rather shocking.

    Source: Wendt, John "Dictionary Use by Language Students," *General Language Journal* 3 (2007): 72-101.

3. My fiancée says that if I buy her a huge diamond ring, this would be a sign that I love her. I would like to know if there is a less expensive sign that would be a sure sign of my love for her.

4. When my English friend speaks of a heat wave just because the temperature reaches over 80°, I have to laugh because I come from Thailand, where we have sunshine most of the year. The days when we have to dress warmly are certainly few, and some people wear shorts outside almost every month of the year.

5. The directions on the package read, Open carefully. Add contents to one glass of warm water. Drink just before bedtime.

Semicolons

The semicolon is used most often to combine two related sentences. Once you get used to using the semicolon, you will find that it is a very easy and useful punctuation tool to vary the sentences in your writing.

- Use a semicolon when you want to connect two simple sentences.

- The function of a semicolon is similar to that of a period. However, in order to use a semicolon, there must be a relationship between the sentences.

> Joey loves to play tennis. He has been playing since he was ten years old.

> Joey loves to play tennis; he has been playing since he was ten years old.

Both sentence pairs are correct. The main difference is that the semicolon in the second example signals the relationship between the ideas in the two sentences. Notice also that *he* is not capitalized in the second example.

ACTIVITY 6

The following sentences use periods for separation. Rewrite the sentences. Replace the periods with semicolons and make any other necessary changes.

1. Gretchen and Bob have been friends since elementary school. They are also next-door neighbors.

   _____

2. The test was complicated. No one passed it.

   _____

3. Tomatoes are necessary for a garden salad. Peas are not.

   _____

4. Mexico lies to the south of the United States. Canada lies to the north.

   _____

ACTIVITY 7

Look at a copy of an English newspaper or magazine. Circle all the semicolons on a page. The number should be relatively small.

NOTE: If the topic of the article is technical or complex, there is a greater chance of finding semicolons. Semicolons are not usually used in informal or friendly writing. Thus, you might see a semicolon in an article about heart surgery or educational research, but not in an ad for a household product or an e-mail or text message to a friend.

Editing for Errors

ACTIVITY 8

Find the 14 punctuation errors in this paragraph and make corrections above the errors.

Example Paragraph 84

An Unexpected Storm

Severe weather is a constant possibility all over the globe; but we never really expect our own area to be affected However last night was different At about ten o'clock a tornado hit Lucedale This violent weather destroyed nine homes near the downtown area In addition to these nine houses that were completely destroyed many others in the area had heavy damage Amazingly no one was injured in last nights terrible storm Because of the rapid reaction of state and local weather watchers most of the areas residents saw the warnings that were broadcast on television

ACTIVITY 9

Find the 15 punctuation errors in this paragraph and make corrections above the errors.

Example Paragraph 85

Deserts

Deserts are some of the most interesting places on earth A desert is not just a dry area it is an area that receives less than ten inches of rainfall a year About one-fifth of the earth is composed of deserts Although many people believe that deserts are nothing but hills of sand this is not true In reality deserts have large rocks mountains canyons and even lakes For instance only about ten percent of the Sahara Desert the largest desert on the earth is sand

Find the 15 punctuation errors in this paragraph and make corrections above the errors.

A Review

I Wish I Could Have Seen His Face Marilyn Kings latest novel is perhaps her greatest triumph In this book King tells the story of the Lamberts a poor family that struggles to survive despite numerous hardships. The Lambert family consists of five strong personalities. Michael Lambert has trouble keeping a job and Naomi earns very little as a maid at a hotel The three children range in age from nine to sixteen. Dan Melinda and Zeke are still in school This well-written novel allows us to step into the conflict that each of the children has to deal with. Only a writer as talented as King could develop five independent characters in such an outstanding manner The plot has many unexpected turns and the outcome of this story will not disappoint readers While King has written several novels that won international praise *I Wish I Could Have Seen His Face* is in many ways better than any of her previous works.

Additional Grammar Activities
Verb Tense

Fill in the blanks with the verb that best completes the sentence. Be sure to use the correct form of the verb. Use the following verbs: *like, cut, break, stir,* and *spread.*

A Simple Sandwich

Making a tuna salad sandwich is not difficult. Put two cans of flaked tuna in a medium-sized bowl. With a fork, _____ the fish apart. _____ up a large white onion or two small yellow onions. _____ in one-third cup of mayonnaise. Then add salt and pepper to taste. Some people _____ to mix pieces of boiled eggs into their salad. Once you finish making the salad, _____ it between two slices of bread. Now you are ready to eat your easy-to-make treat.

ACTIVITY 2

Fill in the blanks with the correct form of any appropriate verb.

Example Paragraph 88

Who Killed Kennedy?

One of the most infamous moments in U.S. history _____ in 1963. In that year, President John F. Kennedy _____ assassinated in Dallas, Texas. Since this event, there _____ many theories about what _____ on that fateful day. According to the official U.S. government report, only one man _____ the bullets that _____ President Kennedy. However, even today many people _____ that there _____ several assassins.

ACTIVITY 3

Fill in the blanks with the correct form of any appropriate verb.

Example Paragraph 89

A Routine Routine

I have one of the most boring daily routines of anyone I _____ . Every morning, I _____ at 7:15.1 _____ a shower and _____ dressed. After that, I _____ breakfast and _____ to the office. I _____ from 8:30 to 4:30. Then I _____ home. This _____ five days a week without fail. Just for once, I wish something different would happen!

Fill in the blanks with the correct form of the verbs in parentheses.

Example Paragraph 90

The Shortest Term in the White House

William Henry Harrison (be) _____ the ninth president of the United States. His presidency was extremely brief. In fact, Harrison (be) _____ president for only one month. He (take) _____ office on March 4,1841. Unfortunately he (catch) _____ a cold that (become) _____ pneumonia. On April 4, Harrison (die) _____ . He (become) _____ the first American president to die while in office. Before becoming president, Harrison (study) _____ to become a doctor and later (serve) _____ in the army.

ACTIVITY 5

Fill in the blanks with the correct form of the verbs in parentheses.

Example Paragraph 91

The History of Brownsville

Brownsville, Texas, is a city with an interesting history. Brownsville (be) _____ originally a fort during the Mexican-American War. During that war, American and Mexican soldiers (fight) _____ several battles in the area around the city. As a matter of fact, the city (get) _____ its name from Major Jacob Brown, an American soldier who was killed in a battle near the old fort. However, Brownsville's history (be) _____ not only connected to war. After the war, the city was best known for farming. The area's rich soil (help) _____ it become a thriving agriculture center. Over time, the agricultural industry (grow) _____ , and today Brownsville farmers (be) _____ well-known for growing cotton and citrus. In sum, both the Mexican-American War and farming have played important historical roles in making Brownsville such an interesting city.

Articles

Fill in the blanks with the correct article. If no article is required, write an X in the blank.

Example Paragraph 92

_____ Simple Math Problem

There is _____ interesting mathematics brainteaser that always amazes _____ people when they first hear it. First, pick _____ number from _____ 1 to _____ 9. Subtract _____ 5. (You may have a negative number.) Multiply this answer by _____ 3. Now square _____ number. Then add _____ digits of _____ number. For _____ example, if your number is 81, add 8 and 1 to get an answer of _____ 9. If _____ number is less than _____ 5, add _____ 5. If _____ number is not less than _____ 5, subtract _____ 4. Now multiply this number by _____ 2. Finally, subtract _____ 6. If you have followed _____ steps correctly, _____ your answer is _____ 4.

Fill in the blanks with the correct article. If no article is required, write an X in the blank.

Example Paragraph 93

_____ Geography Problems among _____ American Students

Are _____ American high school students _____ less educated in _____ geography than high school students in _____ other countries? According to _____ recent survey of _____ high school students all over _____ globe, _____ U.S. students do not know very much about _____ geography. For _____

example, _____ surprisingly large number did not know

_____ capital of _____ state in which

they live. Many could not find _____ Mexico on a map

even though Mexico is one of _____ two countries

that share _____ border with _____

United States. Some _____ educators blame this lack of

_____ geographical knowledge on the move away from

memorization of material that has taken _____ place

in _____ recent years in American schools. Regardless

of _____ cause, the unfortunate fact appears to be that

American _____ high school students are not learning

enough about this subject area.

Fill in the blanks with the correct article. If no article is required, write an X in the blank.

Example Paragraph 94

_____ Homeowners Saving _____ Money with a New Free Service

People who are concerned that their monthly electricity

bill is too high can now take _____ advantage of

_____ special free service offered by the local electricity

company. _____ company will do _____

home energy audit on any house to find out if _____

house is wasting _____ valuable energy. Homeowners

can call _____ power company to schedule _____

convenient time for _____ energy analyst to visit

their home. The audit takes only about _____ hour.

_____ analyst will inspect _____

home and identify potential energy-saving _____

improvements. For _____ example, he or she will

check _____ thermostat, the air-conditioning, and

_____ seals around doors and windows. The major

energy-use _____ problems will be identified, and

_____ analyst will recommend _____

ways to use _____ energy more efficiently.

Fill in the blanks with the correct article. If no article is required, write an X in the blank.

_____ Great Teacher

To this day, I am completely convinced that _____ main reason that I did so well in my French class in _____ high school was the incredible teacher that I had, _____ Mrs. Montluzin. I had not studied _____ foreign language before I started _____ Mrs. Montluzin's French class. _____ idea of being able to communicate in a foreign language, especially _____ French, intrigued me, but _____ idea also scared me. _____ French seemed so difficult at first. We had so much _____ vocabulary to memorize, and we had to do _____ exercises to improve our grammar. While it is true that there was _____ great deal of work to do, _____ Mrs. Montluzin always tried her best to make French class very interesting. She also gave us _____ suggestions for learning _____ French, and these helped me a lot. Since this French class, I have studied a few other languages, and my interest in _____ foreign languages today is due to _____ success I had in French class with _____ Mrs. Montluzin.

Fill in the blanks with the correct article. If no article is required, write an X in the blank.

_____ Surprising Statistics on _____ Higher Education in _____ United States

Although _____ United States is a leader in many areas, it is surprising that _____ number of Americans with _____ college degree is not as high as it is in some _____ other countries. Only about 22 percent of

_____ Americans have attended college for four or more

years. To _____ most people, this rather low ratio of one

in five is shocking. Slightly more than _____ 60 percent

of _____ Americans between _____

ages of 25 and 40 have taken some _____ college classes.

Though these numbers are far from what _____ many

people would expect in _____ United States, these

statistics are _____ huge improvement over figures

at _____ turn of _____ last century.

In _____ 1900, only about _____ 8

percent of all Americans even entered _____ college. At

_____ present time, there are about 21 million students

attending _____ college.

Editing for Errors

ACTIVITY 11

This paragraph contains eight errors. They are in word choice (one), article (one), modal* (one), verb tense (one), subject-verb agreement (three), and word order (one). Mark these errors and write the corrections above the errors.

Example Paragraph 97

A Dangerous Driving Problem

Imagine that you are driving your car home from mall or the library. You come to a bend in the road. You decide that you need to slow down a little, so you tap the brake pedal. Much to your surprise, the car does not begin to slow down. You push the brake pedal all the way down to the floor, but still anything happens. There are a few things you can do when your brakes does not work. One was to pump the brakes. If also this fails, you should to try the emergency brake. If this also fail, you should try to shift the car into a lower gear and rub the tires against the curb until the car come to a stop.

*Modals are *can, should, will, must, may,* and *might.* Modals appear before verbs. We do not use *to* between modals and verbs. (*Incorrect:* I should to go with him. *Correct:* I should go with him.) Modals do not have forms that take *-s, -ing,* or *-ed.*

This paragraph contains ten errors. They are in prepositions (three), word order (one), articles (two), and verb tense (four). Mark these errors and write the corrections above the errors.

The Start of My Love of Aquariums

My love of aquariums began a long time ago. Although I got my first fish when I am just seven years old, I can still remember the store, the fish, and salesclerk who waited on me that day. Because I made good grades on my report card, my uncle has rewarded me with a dollar. A few days later, I was finally able to go to the local dime store for spend my money. It was 1965, and dollar could buy a lot. I looked a lot of different things, but I finally chose to buy a fish. We had an old fishbowl at home, so it seems logical with me to get a fish. I must have spent 15 minutes pacing back and forth in front of all the aquariums before I finally choose my fish. It was a green swordtail, or rather, she was a green swordtail. A few weeks later, she gave birth to 20 or 30 baby swordtails. Years later, I can still remember the fish beautiful that got me so interested in aquariums.

This paragraph contains eight errors. They are in prepositions (one), articles (three), word forms (two), verb tense (one), and subject-verb agreement (one). Mark these errors and write the corrections above the errors.

An Effect of Cellphones on Drivers

Cellular phones, can be threat to safety. A recent study for Donald Redelmeier and Robert Tibshirani of the University of Toronto showed that cellular phones pose a risk to drivers. In fact, people who talk on the phone while driving are four time more likely to have an automobile accident than those who do not use the phone while drive. The Toronto researchers studied 699 drivers who had been in an automobile accident while they were using their cellular phones. The researchers concluded that the main reason for the accidents is not that people used one hand for the telephone and only one for driving. Rather, cause of the accidents was usually that the drivers became distracted, angry, or upset by the phone call. The drivers then lost concentration and was more prone to a car accident.

This paragraph contains seven errors. They are in verb tense (one), articles (two), word forms (three), and subject-verb agreement (one). Mark these errors and write the corrections.

Example Paragraph 100

Problems with American Coins

Many foreigners who come to the United States have very hard time getting used to America coins. The denominations of the coins are one, five, ten, 25, and 50 cents, and one dollar. However, people used only the first four regularly. The smallest coin in value is the penny, but it is not the smallest coin in size. The quarter is one-fourth the value of a dollar, but it is not one-fourth as big as a dollar. There is a dollar coin, but no one ever use it. In fact, perhaps the only place to find one is at a bank. All of the coins are silver-colored except for one, the penny. Finally, because value of each coin is not clearly written on the coin as it is in many country, foreigners often experience problems with monetarily transactions.

ACTIVITY 15

This paragraph contains seven errors. They are in word order (one), articles (two), preposition (one), subject-verb agreement (one), and verb tense (two). Mark these errors and write the corrections.

Example Paragraph 101

An Oasis of Silence

Life on this campus can be extremely hectic, so when I want the solitude, I go usually to the fourth floor of the library. The fourth floor has nothing but shelves and shelves of rare books and obscure periodicals. Because there are only a few small tables with some rather uncomfortable wooden chairs and no copy machines in this floor, few people are staying here very long. Students search for a book or periodical, found it, and then take it to a more sociable floor to photocopy the pages or simply browse through the articles. One of my best friends have told me that he does not like this floor that is so special to me. For him, it is a lonely place. For me, however, it is oasis of silence in a land of turmoil, a place where I can read, think, and write in peace.

Citations and Plagiarism

When writing a paragraph or an essay, writers should use their own words for the most part. Sometimes, however, writers want to use ideas that they have read in a book, an article, or on a website or even heard in a speech. It can make the paragraph or essay more interesting, more factual, or more relevant to the reader. For example, if a writer is working on a paragraph about a recent election, he or she may want to use a quotation from a famous politician. In this case, the writer must indicate that the words are not his or her own, but that they came from someone else. Indicating that a writer's words are not original is called **citing**. In academic writing, it is necessary for a writer to cite all sources of information that are not original.

If the information does not come from the writer's head, it must be cited.

Writers who do not—whether intentionally or unintentionally—give credit to the original author are **plagiarizing**, or stealing, someone else's words. **This is academic theft, and most institutions take this very seriously.**

To avoid plagiarism, it is important to use quotes or a paraphrase which includes an in-text citation, and add a reference or bibliography at the end of your writing.

Using Quotes

Quotations are used when a writer wants to keep the source's exact words. See the examples.

✓ The original reference is the source.

✓ The reference itself is the bibliographical reference.

✓ Use quotation marks " " for original words.

✓ The following verbs are often used to introduce quotes.

describes	points out	states
argues	finds	predicts
claims	insists	reports

Examples: Here are three different examples of quoting a sentence from a text.

Original: There is absolutely no empirical evidence – quantitative or qualitative – to support the familiar notion that monolingual dictionaries are better than bilingual dictionaries for understanding and learning L2.

Quote 1: According to Folse (2004), "There is absolutely no empirical evidence – quantitative or qualitative – to support the familiar notion that monolingual dictionaries are better than bilingual dictionaries for understanding and learning L2."

Quote 2: And while instructors continue to push for monolingual dictionaries, "there is absolutely no empirical evidence – quantitative or qualitative – to support the familiar notion that monolingual dictionaries are better than bilingual dictionaries for understanding and learning L2." (Folse, 2004).

Quote 3: As Folse points out, "There is absolutely no empirical evidence – quantitative or qualitative – to support the familiar notion that monolingual dictionaries are better than bilingual dictionaries for understanding and learning L2" (2004).

Reference/Bibliography

Folse, Keith. *Vocabulary Myths: Applying Second Language Research to Classroom Teaching*. Ann Arbor: University of Michigan Press, 2004.

Paraphrasing

Sometimes writers want to paraphrase or summarize outside information. In this case, the same rules still hold true. **If it is not from the writer's head, it must be cited.**

Original: Every year, the town of Vinci, Italy, receives as many as 500,000 visitors—people coming in search of its most famous son, Leonardo.

Paraphrase: Although a small town, Vinci is visited by many tourists because it is the birthplace of Leonardo da Vinci (Herrick, 2009).

Original: This quiet, unimposing hill town is relatively unchanged from the time of Leonardo.

Paraphrase: Herrick (2009) explains that even after 500 years, the town of Vinci has remained pretty much the same.

Reference/Bibliography

Herrick, T. (2009, January 1). Vinci: A Visit to Leonardo's Home Town. *Offbeat Travel*. Retrieved May 1, 2013, from www.offbeattravel.com/vinci-italy-davinci-home.html

Bibliography

At the end of your paragraph or essay, you must list the sources you used. There are several formats (APA, Chicago, or MLA) for documenting your sources. Always check with your instructor before turning in a paper or essay. This bibliography usually includes the author(s), the publication name, the city, the publisher, the publication year, the media type, and the page number or website.

Here are some guidelines for referencing different works:

Source	Include	Example
Book	Name of author, title of book, publication city: publisher, and year of publication	Folse, Keith. *Vocabulary Myths: Applying Second Language Research to Classroom Teaching.* Ann Arbor: University of Michigan Press, 2004.
Online Article	Name of author (if there is one), title of article, name of Web page, date of publication (if there is one), name of website, Accessed date from URL	"Great Website Design," *Website Design Basics*, http://www.websitedesignbasics.com, Accessed June 26, 2013
Website	Name of Web page, date, name of website. Accessed date, URL	"Global Warming 101." *Union of Concerned Scientists*. Accessed December 14, 2012, http://www.ucsusa.org/global_warming/global_warming_101/
Newspaper	Name of author, title of article, name of newspaper, section date, and page numbers	Smith, Steven, "What To Do in Case of Emergencies." *USA Today*, December 13, 2008, 2–3.
Speech/Interview	Name of author, title of speech or interview, place or course, and date.	Vestri, Elena. Understanding Logical Fallacies. Lecture, ENGL 102, Khalifa University, Abu Dhabi. Feb. 21, 2013.

Academic Word List
Averil Coxhead (2000)

The following words are on the Academic Word List (AWL). The AWL is a list of the 570 highest-frequency academic word families that regularly appear in academic texts. The AWL was compiled by researcher Averil Coxhead based on her analysis of a 3.5 million word corpus.

abandon	available	confirm	detect	evolve
abstract	aware	conflict	deviate	exceed
academy	behalf	conform	device	exclude
access	benefit	consent	devote	exhibit
accommodate	bias	consequent	differentiate	expand
accompany	bond	considerable	dimension	expert
accumulate	brief	consist	diminish	explicit
accurate	bulk	constant	discrete	exploit
achieve	capable	constitute	discriminate	export
acknowledge	capacity	constrain	displace	expose
acquire	category	construct	display	external
adapt	cease	consult	dispose	extract
adequate	challenge	consume	distinct	facilitate
adjacent	channel	contact	distort	factor
adjust	chapter	contemporary	distribute	feature
administrate	chart	context	diverse	federal
adult	chemical	contract	document	fee
advocate	circumstance	contradict	domain	file
affect	cite	contrary	domestic	final
aggregate	civil	contrast	dominate	finance
aid	clarify	contribute	draft	finite
albeit	classic	controversy	drama	flexible
allocate	clause	convene	duration	fluctuate
alter	code	converse	dynamic	focus
alternative	coherent	convert	economy	format
ambiguous	coincide	convince	edit	formula
amend	collapse	cooperate	element	forthcoming
analogy	colleague	coordinate	eliminate	found
analyze	commence	core	emerge	foundation
annual	comment	corporate	emphasis	framework
anticipate	commission	correspond	empirical	function
apparent	commit	couple	enable	fund
append	commodity	create	encounter	fundamental
appreciate	communicate	credit	energy	furthermore
approach	community	criteria	enforce	gender
appropriate	compatible	crucial	enhance	generate
approximate	compensate	culture	enormous	generation
arbitrary	compile	currency	ensure	globe
area	complement	cycle	entity	goal
aspect	complex	data	environment	grade
assemble	component	debate	equate	grant
assess	compound	decade	equip	guarantee
assign	comprehensive	decline	equivalent	guideline
assist	comprise	deduce	erode	hence
assume	compute	define	error	hierarchy
assure	conceive	definite	establish	highlight
attach	concentrate	demonstrate	estate	hypothesis
attain	concept	denote	estimate	identical
attitude	conclude	deny	ethic	identify
attribute	concurrent	depress	ethnic	ideology
author	conduct	derive	evaluate	ignorant
authority	confer	design	eventual	illustrate
automate	confine	despite	evident	image

immigrate	liberal	parameter	reinforce	subsidy
impact	license	participate	reject	substitute
implement	likewise	partner	relax	successor
implicate	link	passive	release	sufficient
implicit	locate	perceive	relevant	sum
imply	logic	percent	reluctance	summary
impose	maintain	period	rely	supplement
incentive	major	persist	remove	survey
incidence	manipulate	perspective	require	survive
incline	manual	phase	research	suspend
income	margin	phenomenon	reside	sustain
incorporate	mature	philosophy	resolve	symbol
index	maximize	physical	resource	tape
indicate	mechanism	plus	respond	target
individual	media	policy	restore	task
induce	mediate	portion	restrain	team
inevitable	medical	pose	restrict	technical
infer	medium	positive	retain	technique
infrastructure	mental	potential	reveal	technology
inherent	method	practitioner	revenue	temporary
inhibit	migrate	precede	reverse	tense
initial	military	precise	revise	terminate
initiate	minimal	predict	revolution	text
injure	minimize	predominant	rigid	theme
innovate	minimum	preliminary	role	theory
input	ministry	presume	route	thereby
insert	minor	previous	scenario	thesis
insight	mode	primary	schedule	topic
inspect	modify	prime	scheme	trace
instance	monitor	principal	scope	tradition
institute	motive	principle	section	transfer
instruct	mutual	prior	sector	transform
integral	negate	priority	secure	transit
integrate	network	proceed	seek	transmit
integrity	neutral	process	select	transport
intelligent	nevertheless	professional	sequence	trend
intense	nonetheless	prohibit	series	trigger
interact	norm	project	sex	ultimate
intermediate	normal	promote	shift	undergo
internal	notion	proportion	significant	underlie
interpret	notwithstanding	prospect	similar	undertake
interval	nuclear	protocol	simulate	uniform
intervene	objective	psychology	site	unify
intrinsic	obtain	publication	so-called	unique
invest	obvious	publish	sole	utilize
investigate	occupy	purchase	somewhat	valid
invoke	occur	pursue	source	vary
involve	odd	qualitative	specific	vehicle
isolate	offset	quote	specify	version
issue	ongoing	radical	sphere	via
item	option	random	stable	violate
job	orient	range	statistic	virtual
journal	outcome	ratio	status	visible
justify	output	rational	straightforward	vision
label	overall	react	strategy	visual
labor	overlap	recover	stress	volume
layer	overseas	refine	structure	voluntary
lecture	panel	regime	style	welfare
legal	paradigm	region	submit	whereas
legislate	paragraph	register	subordinate	whereby
levy	parallel	regulate	subsequent	widespread

Useful Vocabulary for Better Writing

These useful words and phrases can help you write better sentences and paragraphs. Many are found in the *Great Writing 2: Great Paragraphs* model paragraphs, and they can make your writing sound more academic, natural, and fluent.

Giving and Adding Examples

Words and Phrases	Examples
For example, S + V / *For instance,* S + V	Our reading teacher assigns a lot of homework. *For example,* last night we had to read ten pages and write an essay.
The first reason + VERB	The article we read in class gave three reasons that our planet is in trouble. *The first reason* is about the increasing population.

Concluding Sentences

Words and Phrases	Examples
In conclusion, S + V	*In conclusion,* I believe everyone should vote in every election.
By doing all of these things, S + V	*By doing all of these things,* we can improve education in our country.
Because of this, S + V	*Because of this,* many people will have better health care.
As a result, S + V	*As a result,* I chose to go to college in France instead of my country.
For these reasons, S + V	*For these reasons,* I prefer to eat at home instead of a restaurant.
In sum, S + V / *In summary,* S + V / *To summarize ,* S + V	*In sum,* World War II was a very complicated war with many countries fighting for very different reasons, but in many ways, it was a continuation of World War I.
In other words, S + V	*In other words,* the judge made an incorrect decision.
From the information given, we can conclude that S + V	*From the information given, we can conclude that* Mark Johnson is certainly the best soccer player in this decade.
It is clear that S + V	*It is clear that* exercising every day improved your health.

Comparing

Words and Phrases	Examples
NOUN *is* COMPARATIVE ADJECTIVE *than* NOUN	New York *is larger than* Rhode Island.
S + V + COMPARATIVE ADVERB *than* Y.	The cats ran *faster than* the dogs.
S + V. *In comparison,* S + V.	Canada has provinces. *In comparison,* Brazil has states.
Although NOUN *and* NOUN *are similar in* NOUN, S + V	*Although* France *and* Spain *are similar in* size, they are different in many ways.
NOUN *and* NOUN *are similar.*	Brazil *and* the United States *are* surprisingly *similar.*
NOUN *is the same*	Our house *is the same* size as your house.
…as ADJECTIVE *as…*	Our house is *as big as* your house.
Like NOUN, NOUN *also*	*Like* Brazil, Mexico *also* has states.
both NOUN *and* NOUN…	*In both* German *and* Japanese, the verb appears at the end of a sentence.

Likewise, S + V / Also, S + V	The blooms on the red roses last longer than most other flowers. *Likewise,* the blooms for the pink rose are long-lasting.
Similarly, S + V …/ Similar to NOUN	Economists believe India has a bright future. *Similarly,* Brazil's future is on a very positive track.

Contrasting

Words and Phrases	Examples
S + V. In contrast, S + V.	*Algeria* is a very large country. *In contrast,* the UAE is very small.
Contrasted with / In contrast to NOUN	*In contrast to* last year, our company has doubled its profits this year.
Although / Even though / Though S + V	*Although* Spain and France are similar in size, they are different in many other ways.
Unlike NOUN,	*Unlike* the pink roses, the red roses are very expensive.
However, S + V	Canada has provinces. *However,* Brazil has states.
One the one hand, S + V *On the other hand,* S + V	*On the one hand,* Maggie loved to travel. *On the other hand,* she hated to be away from her home.
The opposite S + V	Most of the small towns in my state are experiencing a boom in tourism. In my hometown, *the opposite* is true.
NOUN *and* NOUN *are different.*	My older brother *and* my younger brother *are very different.*

Telling a Story / Narrating

Words and Phrases	Examples
When I was X, I would VERB	*When I was* a child, *I would* go fishing every weekend.
I have never felt so ADJ *in my life.*	*I have never felt so* anxious *in my life.*
I will never forget NOUN	*I will never forget* the day I took my first international flight.
I can still remember NOUN / *I will always remember* NOUN	*I can still remember* the day I started my first job.
NOUN *was the best / worst day of my life.*	My wedding was *the best day of my life.*
Every time X happened, Y happened.	*Every time* I used that computer, I had a problem.
This was my first …	*This was my first* job after graduating from college.

Describing a Process

Words and Phrases	Examples
First (Second, Third, etc.), … *Next,… After that,… Then,…* *Finally,…*	*First,* I cut the apples into small pieces. *Next,* I added some mayonnaise. *After that,* I added some salt. *Finally,* I mixed everything together well.
The first thing you should do is VERB	*The first thing you should do is* turn on the computer.
VERB+*-ing requires you to follow (number) of steps.*	*Saving* a file on a computer *requires you to follow several simple steps.*
Before you VERB, *you should* VERB.	*Before you* write a paragraph, *you should* brainstorm for ideas.
After (When)…	*After* you brainstorm your ideas, you can select the best ones to write about in your essay.

After that, …	*After that,* you can select the best ones to write about in your essay.
The last step is… / Finally, …	*Finally,* you should cook all of the ingredients for an hour.
If you follow these important steps in VERB + *-ing,…*	*If you follow these important steps in* applying for a passport, you will have your new document in a very short time.

Defining

Words and Phrases	Examples
The NOUN, *which is a/an* NOUN + ADJECTIVE CLAUSE, MAIN VERB	An owl, *which is* a bird that has huge round eyes, is awake most of the night.
According to the dictionary…	*According to* The Collins Cobuild Dictionary of American English, gossip is "an informal conversation, often about people's private affairs."
The dictionary definition of NOUN	*The dictionary definition of* gumbo is not very good.
X released a report stating that S + V	*The president's office released a report stating that* the new law will require all adults between the ages of 18 and 30 to serve at least one year of active military duty.
In other words, S + V	*In other words,* we have to redo everything we have done so far.
,…which means…	The paper is due tomorrow, *which means* if you want to get a good grade, you need to finish it today.
NOUN *means…*	Gossip *means* talking or writing about other people's private affairs.

Showing Cause and Effect

Words and Phrases	Examples
Because of NOUN, S + V. *Because* S + V, S + V.	*Because of* the traffic problems, it is easy to see why the city is building a new tunnel.
NOUN *can trigger* NOUN. NOUN *can cause* NOUN.	An earthquake *can trigger* tidal waves and *can cause* massive destruction.
Due to NOUN, …	*Due to* the snowstorm, all schools will be closed tomorrow.
As a result of NOUN…	*As a result of* his efforts, he got a better job.
Therefore,…/ As a result,…/ For this reason,…/ Consequently,…	It suddenly began to rain. *Therefore,* we all got wet.
NOUN *will bring about …*	The use of the Internet *will bring about a* change in education.
NOUN *has had a good / bad effect on…*	Computer technology *has had both positive and negative effects* on society.
The correlation is clear / evident.	*The correlation* between junk food and obesity *is clear.*

Describing

Words and Phrases	Examples
Prepositions of location: *above, across, around, in the dark, near, under...*	The children raced their bikes *around* the school.
Descriptive adjectives: *wonderful, delightful, dangerous, informative, rusty...*	The *bent, rusty* bike squeaked when I rode it.
SUBJECT *is* ADJECTIVE.	This dictionary *is informative*.
X is the most ADJECTIVE + NOUN.	To me, Germany *is the most interesting* country in Europe.
X tastes / looks / smells / feels like NOUN.	My ID card *looks like* a credit card.
X is known / famous for its NOUN.	France *is known for* its cheese.

Stating an Opinion

Words and Phrases	Examples
Without a doubt, VERB *is* ADJECTIVE *idea / method / decision / way.*	*Without a doubt,* walking to work each day *is* an excellent *way* to lose weight.
Personally, I believe/think/feel/agree/ disagree/ suppose S + V.	*Personally, I believe that* smoking on a bus should not be allowed.
VERB+*-ing should not be allowed.*	Smoking in public *should not be allowed.*
In my opinion/ view/ experience, NOUN	*In my opinion,* smoking is rude.
For this reason, S + V. */ That is why I think...*	I do not have a car. *For this reason,* I do not care about rising gasoline prices.
There are many benefits / advantages to NOUN.	*There are many benefits* to swimming every day.
There are many drawbacks / disadvantages to NOUN.	*There are many drawbacks to* eating your meals at a restaurant.
I am convinced that S + V	*I am convinced that* education at a university should be free to all citizens.
NOUN *should be required / mandatory.*	College *should be required.*
I prefer NOUN *to* NOUN.	*I prefer* soccer to football.
To me, banning / prohibiting NOUN *makes (perfect) sense.*	*To me, banning* cell phones while driving *makes perfect sense.*
For all of these important reasons, I think / believe / feel (that) S + V	*For all of these important reasons, I think* smoking *should be* banned in public.
Based on X, I have come to the conclusion that S + V	*Based on* two books that I read recently, *I have come to the conclusion that* global warming is the most serious problem that my generation faces.

Arguing and Persuading

Words and Phrases	Examples
It is important to remember that S + V	*It is important to remember* that school uniforms would only be worn during school hours.
According to a recent survey, S + V	*According to a recent survey,* 85 percent of high school students felt they had too much homework.
Even more important, S + V	*Even more important,* statistics show the positive effects that school uniforms have on behavior.
Despite this, S + V	The report says this particular kind of airplane is dangerous. *Despite this,* the government has not banned this airplane.
SUBJECT *must / should / ought to* VERB	Researchers *must* stop unethical animal testing.
The reason for S + V	*The reason for* people's support of this plan is that it provides equal treatment for all citizens.
To emphasize, S + V	*To emphasize,* I support a lower age for voting but only for those who already have a high school diploma.
For these reasons, S + V	*For these reasons,* public schools should require uniforms.
Obviously, S + V	*Obviously,* there are many people who would disagree with what I have just said.
Without a doubt, S + V	*Without a doubt,* students ought to learn a foreign language.
I agree that S + V. *However* S + V	*I agree that* a college degree is important. *However,* getting a practical technical license can also be very useful.

Reacting/Responding

Words and Phrases	Examples
TITLE *by* AUTHOR *is a / an...*	*Harry Potter and the Goblet of Fire by* J.K. Rowling *is an* entertaining book to read.
My first reaction to the prompt / news / article was / is NOUN.	*My first reaction to the article was* fear.
When I read / look at / think about NOUN, *I was amazed / shocked / surprised ...*	*When I read* the article, *I was surprised* to learn of his athletic ability.

Appendices

Appendix 1

Building Better Sentences

Being a good writer involves many skills, such as being able to write with correct grammar, use variety in vocabulary selection, and state ideas concisely. A good writer also learns to create longer, more detailed sentences from simple ideas. Study the short sentences below.

The time was yesterday.

It was afternoon.

There was a storm.

The storm was strong.

The movement of the storm was quick.

The storm moved toward the coast.

The coast was in North Carolina.

Notice that every sentence has an important piece of information. A good writer would not write all these sentences separately. Instead, the most important information from each sentence can be used to create ONE longer, coherent sentence.

Read the sentences again; this time, the important information has been circled.

The time was yesterday.

It was afternoon.

There was a storm.

The movement of the storm was quick.

The storm moved toward the coast.

The coast was in North Carolina.

Here are some strategies for taking the circled information and creating a new sentence.

1. Create time phrases to introduce or end a sentence: yesterday + afternoon

2. Find the key noun: storm

3. Find key adjectives: strong

4. Create noun phrases: a strong + storm

5. Change word forms: movement = move; quick = quickly

                moved + quickly

6. Create prepositional phrases: toward the coast,

                toward the coast (of North Carolina)

                      or

                toward the North Carolina coast

Now read this improved, longer sentence:

Yesterday afternoon, a strong storm moved quickly toward the North Carolina coast.

Here are some additional strategies for building better sentences:

7. Use coordinating conjunctions (*and, but, or, nor, yet, for, so*) to connect two sets of ideas.

8. Use subordinating conjunctions, such as *after, while, since,* and *because,* to connect related ideas.

9. Use clauses with relative pronouns, such as *who, which, that,* and *whose,* to describe or define a noun or noun phrase.

10. Use pronouns to refer to previously mentioned information.

11. Use possessive adjectives and pronouns, such as *my, her, his, ours,* and *theirs.* These words can make your writing flow more smoothly.

   Study the following example.

   (Susan) (went) somewhere. That place was (the mall.) Susan wanted to (buy new shoes.) The shoes were for (Susan's mother.)

   Now read the improved, longer sentence:

   Susan went to the mall because she wanted to buy new shoes for her mother.

Practices

This section contains practices for the example paragraphs in Units 1–10. Follow these steps for each practice:

1. Read the sentences. Circle the most important information in each sentence.

2. Write an original sentence from the information you circled. Use the strategies listed above.

Practice 1 Unit 1

A.

1. An (egg salad sandwich) is one of the (easiest foods to make.)

2. An egg salad sandwich is one of the (most delicious foods to make.)

3. This is for (lunch.)

   An egg salad sandwich is one of the easiest and most delicious foods to make for lunch.

B.

1. Brazil is near Chile.

2. Chile is near Brazil.

3. Brazil and Chile are different in geography.

4. Brazil and Chile are different in population.

5. Brazil and Chile are different in language.

   Brazil and Chile are diffrent.

C.

1. First, boil eggs.

2. There are two eggs.

3. Do this for five minutes.

Practice 2 Unit 1

A.

    1. I was 23 years old at the time.

    2. I had just graduated.

    3. The graduation was from college.

B.

    1. Chile and Brazil are two countries.

    2. Chile is important.

    3. Brazil is important.

    4. They are in South America.

C.

    1. Jim Thorpe won medals.

    2. The medals were Olympic medals.

    3. They were gold medals.

    4. He won them in 1912.

    5. He was not allowed to keep the medals.

Practice 3 Unit 2

A.

    1. Mimi is a teacher.

    2. She teaches kindergarten.

    3. She is a teacher at a school.

    4. The school is King Elementary School.

B.

1. She teaches children.

2. The children are very young.

3. There are 22 children.

_____

_____

C.

1. Mimi must attend meetings.

2. Mimi must create lessons.

3. The lessons are new.

4. Mimi must do this after school.

_____

_____

Practice 4 Unit 3

A.

1. The season is winter.

2. This season is the best.

3. This season is for kids.

_____

_____

B.

1. This dictionary contains words.

2. The dictionary is monolingual.

3. There are more than 42,000 words.

_____

_____

C.

1. The crash of a jet baffled investigators.

2. The crash was shocking.

3. The jet was a 747 jumbo jet.

4. The crash was off the coast of New York.

_____

_____

Practice 5 Unit 3

A.

1. Research has confirmed that eating vegetables, such as broccoli, may reduce the risk of some types of cancer.

2. The research is recent.

3. The vegetables are dark green ones.

4. The vegetables are leafy vegetables.

5. Another example of this is cabbage.

_____

_____

B.

1. Research suggests that studying music can improve a person's brain function.

2. Research suggests that studying music can improve a person's intelligence.

3. There is a great deal of the research.

_____

_____

C.

1. A heart is necessary for life.

2. The heart is good.

3. The heart is strong.

4. The life is long.

5. The life is healthy.

_____

_____

Practice 6 Unit 3

A.

1. Malaysia is a country.

2. Thailand is a country.

3. These two countries are in Asia.

4. They are in Southeast Asia.

_____

_____

B.

1. Malaysia has beaches.
2. There are miles of beaches.
3. The beaches are beautiful.
4. These beaches attract tourists.
5. This is true about Thailand, too.

_____

_____

C.

1. Students can choose to major in art.
2. They are at a university.
3. Only a small number choose to major in this subject.
4. This number is low for a reason.
5. The reason is that they are concerned about job possibilities.
6. The job possibilities are in the future.

_____

_____

Practice 7 Unit 4

A.

1. One of the cities to visit is Washington, D.C.
2. It is one of the best cities.
3. It is on a coast of the United States.
4. The coast is in the east.

_____

_____

B.

1. The area consists of over two million square feet.
2. The area belongs to the Grand Palace.
3. The wall is more than 6,000 feet long.
4. This wall surrounds the palace.

_____

_____

C.

    1. Texas is home to snakes.

    2. There are several kinds of snakes.

    3. These snakes are poisonous.

_____

_____

Practice 8 Unit 4

A.

    1. Music is popular.

    2. The music is soft.

    3. It is popular because it helps students.

    4. It helps students sleep better.

_____

_____

B.

    1. Giraffes have eyelashes to protect their eyes.

    2. The eyelashes are thick.

    3. They protect their eyes from dust.

    4. The dust is in their habitat.

    5. Their habitat is dry.

_____

_____

C.

    1. Students learn that North America and South America are one continent.

    2. They call this the Americas.

_____

_____

Practice 9 Unit 5

A.

    1. Only tourists attempt to cross the bridge.

    2. The tourists are adventure-seeking.

    3. The bridge is narrow and swinging.

    4. This happens today.

_____

_____

B.

    1. Hockey is a sport.

    2. It is a popular sport.

    3. It is popular in Canada.

    4. It is popular in the United States.

_____

_____

C.

    1. Teh tarikh is a beverage.

    2. Teh tarikh is popular.

    3. Teh tarikh is served in restaurants.

    4. Teh tarikh is served in markets.

    5. These restaurants and markets are in Southeast Asian countries.

    6. Examples of these countries are Malaysia and Singapore.

_____

_____

Practice 10 Unit 5

A.

    1. Coins were left under the mast.

    2. The mast was part of the ship.

    3. There were a small number of coins.

    4. This happened when a new ship was built.

_____

_____

B.

  1. Scientists find evidence of this tradition.
  2. The evidence is in a variety of locations.
  3. The tradition is long-standing.
  4. This happens today.

  _____

  _____

C.

  1. Floods provided the marsh with water to support its plants and animals.
  2. These floods always did this.
  3. The water was new.
  4. The marsh had a wide variety of plants and animals.

  _____

  _____

Practice 11 Unit 6

A.

  1. The pretzel became popular.
  2. This event happened rapidly.
  3. This event happened throughout Europe.

  _____

  _____

B.

  1. Pretzels were made in a monastery.
  2. They were the first pretzels made.
  3. It was an Italian monastery.
  4. This happened in A.D. 610.

  _____

  _____

C.

1. The pretzel is a snack.

2. It is especially popular.

3. This is true in Germany.

4. This is true in Austria.

5. This is true in the United States.

6. It is true today.

_____

_____

Practice 12 Unit 6

A.

1. A hurricane is a storm.

2. The storm is dangerous.

3. The storm features winds and rain.

4. The winds are high.

5. The rains are heavy.

_____

_____

B.

1. A hurricane resulted in thousands of deaths.

2. The hurricane surprised the residents of Galveston, Texas.

3. This happened in 1900.

_____

_____

C.

1. A folly is an action.

2. This action is costly.

3. The action has a result.

4. The result is bad or absurd.

_____

_____

Practice 13 Unit 7

A.

1. Keeping a vocabulary notebook is not complicated to do.
2. The notebook is for learning words.
3. The words are English.
4. The words are new.
5. This statement is true if you follow a few steps.
6. The steps are easy.

_____

_____

B.

1. You should follow these directions.
2. The directions are simple.
3. Eating a taco can be an experience.
4. The experience is less messy.

_____

_____

C.

1. I am going to explain the steps.
2. The steps are to do a math trick.
3. The math trick is really interesting.
4. I learned the trick yesterday.
5. The trick will amaze your friends.

_____

_____

Practice 14 Unit 7

A.

1. Hit the ball into the box.
2. The box is small.
3. It is on the opposite side of the net.

_____

_____

B.

1. The racket should be near your knee.

2. The racket is yours.

3. It is the knee on the left.

4. Do this after you have completed your serve.

_____

_____

C.

1. You will need a quart jar.

2. The jar must be clean.

3. The jar must have a tight lid.

4. You will need some tape.

5. You will need a goldfish.

6. You will need some water.

7. You will need a few plants.

8. The plants need to be green.

9. You need all this for the experiment.

_____

_____

Practice 15 Unit 8

A.

1. A mother is standing.

2. She is to your left.

3. Her child is standing.

4. The child is crying.

_____

_____

B.

1. The tornado used its power to uproot trees.

2. The tornado used its power to toss cars around.

3. The trees were huge.

4. The cars were tossed around as if they were toys.

_____

_____

C.

    1. Mother also trimmed the flowers.

    2. She did this to make room for their replacements.

    3. The flowers were old.

    4. Their replacements were bright.

_____

_____

Practice 16 Unit 8

A.

    1. The trees are gray.

    2. The trees are brittle.

    3. The trees are old.

    4. The trees are near the river.

_____

_____

B.

    1. A cat is curled up in a ball.

    2. The cat is fat.

    3. The cat is striped.

    4. The cat has whiskers.

    5. The whiskers are long.

    6. The cat is on the right side of the sofa.

_____

_____

C.

    1. The Statue of Liberty has a crown on her head.

    2. The crown has seven spikes.

    3. These spikes symbolize the oceans and the continents.

    4. There are seven oceans.

    5. There are seven continents.

_____

_____

Practice 17 Unit 9

A.

    1. I am in favor of a ban.

    2. The ban is on cell phone use.

    3. This use is by drivers.

    4. I am in favor of a ban because cell phones and driving are a deadly mix.

    _____

    _____

B.

    1. Texting is certainly very common.

    2. This fact is true now.

    3. This is because texting is convenient.

    4. This is because texting is fast.

    _____

    _____

C.

    1. School uniforms should be mandatory.

    2. This should be for all students.

    3. This is for a number of reasons.

    _____

    _____

Practice 18 Unit 9

A.

    1. Too much time can cause damage.

    2. The time is in the sun.

    3. The damage is to the skin.

    4. The damage is severe.

    5. This occurs especially in young children.

    _____

    _____

B.

1. She parked a car.
2. It was her car.
3. She parked illegally.
4. She got a ticket.
5. The ticket was for $50.

_____

_____

C.

1. One source is the newspaper.
2. The source is good.
3. It is for topics.
4. The topics are for paragraphs.
5. The paragraphs are opinion paragraphs.

_____

_____

Practice 19 Unit 10

A.

1. I practiced my speech.
2. I did this with my notes.
3. I did this in front of a mirror.
4. I did this in front of my cat.
5. I did this in front of my husband.

_____

_____

B.

1. Everything changed.
2. This happened when I was 16 years old.
3. This happened because my parents decided to move.
4. The move was to Florida.

_____

_____

C.

    1. I was in a building.

    2. I was on the third floor.

    3. It was a six-story building.

    4. I thought the building was going to collapse.

_____

_____

Practice 20 Unit 10

A.

    1. The man waited until a guard gave him a number.

    2. He did this patiently.

    3. The number was to enter the building.

    4. The building was warm.

_____

_____

B.

    1. He gathered the paperwork.

    2. The paperwork was important.

    3. The paperwork included his I-20 document.

    4. The paperwork included his passport.

    5. The paperwork included his bank statements.

    6. The paperwork included even a letter.

    7. The letter was from his doctor.

_____

_____

_____

C.

    1. My best friend was sitting on a train.

    2. I was sitting on a train.

    3. The train was in Frankfurt.

    4. The train was bound for Paris.

    5. This is when the nightmare began.

_____

_____

Appendix 2

Peer Editing Sheet Sample

This is an example of the Peer Editing Sheets available for *Great Writing 2: Great Paragraphs*. To print them out, go to NGL.Cengage.com/GW2.

Unit 1

Writer: _____ Date: _____

Peer Editor: _____

1. What is the general topic of the paragraph? _____

   Does the title relate to this general topic?   ❑ yes   ❑ no

2. What is the more specific topic? _____

   _____

3. If you can find the topic sentence, write it here. _____

   _____

4. How many sentences does the paragraph have? _____ Do all the sentences relate to the

   same topic?   ❑ yes   ❑ no   If any sentence is not about the topic, write it here.

   _____

   _____

5. Can you understand the meaning of every sentence?   ❑ yes   ❑ no   If you answered *no*, write the

   unclear sentence(s) here.

   _____

   _____

6. Does every sentence have a verb?   ❑ yes   ❑ no   If any sentence does not have a verb, write that

   sentence here and add a verb.

   _____

   _____

   _____

7. Is the paragraph indented? ❑ yes ❑ no If you answered *no*, circle the area where it should be indented.

8. Are any key nouns repeated? ❑ yes ❑ no If so, give an example.

_____

_____

9. If you have ideas or suggestions for making the paragraph better, write them here.

_____

_____

_____

Index